101

*inspirational quotes **for Us***

RICH
CHICKS

Life Is Rich When You Are
Able to Acknowledge That . . .

A n d r é e   N i c o l e

Library of Congress Control Number: 2014920924
ISBN: Hardcover   978-1-5035-1990-9
                 Softcover   978-1-5035-1991-6
                 eBook   978-1-5035-1992-3

Rev. date: 01/20/2015

To order additional copies of this book, contact:
Xlibris
1-888-795-4274
www.Xlibris.com
Orders@Xlibris.com
672745

101

inspirational quotes for Us

RICH
CHICKS

To my mother and grandmothers, who are not only beautiful but courageous women. For they have taught me everything I know to be rich.

This book is also for all the Rich Chicks because you too truly exemplify the epitome of strength! My wish is for your once "silenced dialogue" to be transformed into a powerful voice that will now inform, inspire, and allow others to believe. You are not only Rich Chicks but are true gems, and I will continue to applaud you all for never giving up on searching for your inward treasures.

To my father, my husband, my son, and everyone else who supported me throughout this RICH journey, thank you.

The greatest
good you can do
for another is not
just share your
riches but
reveal to them
their own.

—Benjamin Disraeli

Life is RICH when you are able to acknowledge that . . .

Inspiration begins to bubble when you have seen the bottom.

It has been almost four years since the time of my motor vehicle accident. And although it has been quite a journey, those single steps of fear and having the opportunity to have been invited to unwillingly see the bottom of despair motivated me to do most of the things that I had wanted to do for many years.

I began writing more of my thoughts and recording them down in hopes of seeing it come into fruition. I began appreciating the small things in life again, and doing the things that I always wanted to do. Whether it was becoming a certified life and wellness coach, attending various functions and being able to network with some amazing people, being invited as a guest speaker at various events and sharing my story and vision of the benefits of believing in your dreams. Or merely going for long walks and being able to take in all the sights, sounds and even the smells. I found that participating in those things kept me grounded and therefore opened for newfound beginnings—beginnings that I now know were brought on by mere inspiration of these moments during *my* time of having to relearn how to be still.

In doing so, I was able to create a brand and a business that would eventually be used as a platform to inspire women to feel stronger, braver, and more beautiful inside and out. This encouraged me to speak to issues addressing health, wellness, and financial stability because of what I experienced during the years and after my motor vehicle accident.

For most of my days that bubbling inspiration factor to do something creative and out of the box allowed me to transform something negative and dark into something that was so positive and full of light. I wanted to have that opportunity to assist others and allow them to equip their rich inward treasures, heal, and ultimately become whole. Being able to do that for others continues to be extremely important to me because of the fact that my eyes had seen so much.

This inspiration has lead me onto a path of continual self-reflection, which allowed me to have a much better understanding of why individuals who have spoken from a place that required them to experience every emotion have become happier, more appreciative, more passionate, and most importantly, at peace with themselves.

In doing so, I traveled the directions my journeys have allowed me to go. Furthermore, the new things that I have been able to *see* have given me a wealth of experience and also a brand-new voice—just because I have seen the bottom.

Rich thoughts

Who or what inspires you to be the best that you can be?

_____

_____

_____

_____

_____

_____

_____

_____

_____

_____

_____

_____

Rich Point for Your Day

Today I will be inspired to use by darkest moments as an anchorage of a source of positive inspiration.

Life is RICH when you are able to acknowledge that . . .

Failure is success turned inside out.

I remember having conversations with my son about the necessity of trying, trying some more, and then trying again when at first he was unable to succeed. For if he never attempted to give it his all, how could he possible know about all the hidden talents that he possessed? Furthermore, how would he know how close he would have been in accomplishing those goals and dreams if he did not put forth his best foot?

Unfortunately in today's society we have become quite impatient. From the creation of microwavable dinners that can be made in less than five minutes to having access to everything and anything we want with just the click of the mouse, this generation wants things done in such a quick manner that they have forgotten how important it is to exercise patience. If we attempt to do something, we often have no time for any failures. For we want to succeed the first time when we are given the opportunity to do so. We do not even want to entertain the thought of having to try a first, second, or third time in order to fulfill the goal that we are aiming for.

Although many of these conversations that I had with my son where directed and meant for him to understand the true meaning of never giving up, I quickly learned that they were valuable lessons and reminders for me. These discussions allowed me to reflect upon the importance of having the ability to experience, go through, and conquer these trials, tests, and tribulations in any area of our life with fierce determination and drive.

These failures became so fitting to *my* life because they were only little distractions that were thrown unexpectedly my way that allowed myself to create my most meaningful, creative, and purposeful masterpieces.

My eyes had failed to see and fully comprehend at that time that, when things were not go according to plan, this is where I learned some of the best life lessons.

I later realized that failure is merely success turned inside out.

Rich thoughts

Have you ever felt to give up the first time you did not succeed at something you set out to accomplish?

_____

_____

_____

_____

_____

_____

_____

_____

_____

_____

_____

_____

Rich Point for Your Day

Today I will be successful by realizing that it is okay to fail and not succeed upon the first try.

Life is RICH when you are able to acknowledge that . . .

To be RICH means to be whole in every facet of your life.

I find that within our society we are all too caught up with the materialistic acquisition of wealth. Whether you feel the importance of having to keep up with the Joneses, and you find yourself purchasing that enormous house with the ridiculous amount of bedrooms and bathrooms because that is how you define being rich; or perhaps you equate one's richness with the fancy and expensive cars that sit pretty on the driveway or are parked up in your garage; or perhaps it is the neighborhood that you purposely chose to reside in because of the prestigious or affluent association with that town or city—your definition or the notion of what constitutes richness can also be found in your choice of schools for your children to attend that academic school year.

Sad but true. These people have bought into this notion of wealth acquisition and define it solely on the basis of how much one has or how they *look* to others. Don't get me wrong. Nothing is wrong with having the finer things in life. However, what they fail to realize is that, when one is filled with the richness of being whole, one begins to go down the path of self-reflection that leads to other routes that consist of the occasional rocky paths. These detours do allow one to be refreshed and hence ultimately lead one to the right path of restoration.

One can have everything yet have nothing at the same time if that richness is not discovered, fulfilled, and maintained. Being whole in every facet of one's life is the best way to delineate the concept of richness. And although much is easier said than done, this remains to be a continuous work in progress and is very much an integral part of my life, and therefore, I continue to work toward fueling and maintaining the fire to be rich as long as I can.

Rich thoughts

Was there ever a time when you were broken? What led you down that path of brokenness?

———————————————————————————
———————————————————————————
———————————————————————————
———————————————————————————
———————————————————————————
———————————————————————————
———————————————————————————
———————————————————————————
———————————————————————————
———————————————————————————
———————————————————————————

Rich Point for Your Day

Today I will be rich by realizing that being sound in mind, body, and spirit is the component of being whole.

Life is RICH when you are able to acknowledge that . . .

Simplicity is DELICIOUS.

Although I do like the finer things in life, I also love the simple things that life has to offer. They say that the best things in life are free, and this is so true. It could be something as simple as admiring the sunrise or sunset, watching the waves crash against the rocks, visiting Niagara Falls, or even simply watching an old flick and having some popcorn layered in butter. For me, enjoying those things enveloped in simplicity is fine with and for me.

The quality or condition of being plain or natural was not always a first option for me. For my life was super delicious in the sense that my weekdays, weeknights, and weekends were always highly amusing, pleasing, or enjoyable. I thought that I had to ALWAYS be busy, whether the busyness consisted of sports-related or family-related activities, dining in a restaurant, partaking in social/family rendezvous, shopping, hanging out with friends or colleagues, attending meetings/conferences, giving lectures, or merely spending time away (just the two of us) at our favorite spots in and around the city. As you can see, my life was truly complex and delicious.

However, I believe that with age also came maturity, and then my priorities of wanting to acquire the grandiose things in life became secondary to none for me.

However, there came a point in time where I began to indulge in the simple pleasures of life again.

Waking up to another blessed day, making someone smile, walking barefoot on the grass, hugging my child and my husband, helping someone in need, on a sunny day lying on my back and looking up at the clouds, at night watching the stars, having pillow fights, dancing as I watch myself in the mirror, telling jokes, or kissing my husband in the rain—these illustrations are just a few of the simple things in my life that I give more attention to and also love to do.

I felt the need to go back to the basics, and in doing so, I took full advantage of the gifts that were present in my life and then relearned how to really celebrate life in *my* own unique way. Needless to say, it was the best thing that I could have ever done because every once in a while it is good to just sit back and smell the flowers.

This took some time—a long time, to be quite frank. But because I had undergone this process, I now appreciate everything and take great pleasure in taking nothing for granted.

Don't get me wrong, I still do all the complex delicious things that I once did before, just not how I used to. I guess all the tests, trials, and tribulations that I encountered and that I had to not only sort through but had to conquer, allowed me to truly be thankful for and be more appreciative of the smaller and simpler things in life. And because of that, life had become that more delicious.

Rich thoughts

Do you appreciate the smaller things in life? How do you show your appreciation?

_____

_____

_____

_____

_____

_____

_____

_____

_____

_____

_____

_____

_____

Rich Point for Your Day

Today I will exercise simplicity by appreciating the small things that go unnoticed within a day so that it may be that more delicious.

Life is RICH when you are able to acknowledge that . . .

It's a beautiful thing to be awakened by the gentle touch of LOVE.

Many health studies point to the importance and benefits that one's touch may have on one's life. Perhaps you have heard about baby twins being placed in the NICU after birth and then learn that one of the twins has no longer responded to any of the treatments. In this given situation, you often see the other healthy twin holding, touching, or comforting their sibling during these crucial times of need.

Perhaps you have also heard of these coma patients who lie in their hospital bed nonresponsive to their surroundings, and because of that familiarity of their family members' touch, they begin to respond in miraculous ways. At times we may read the odd news articles or watch a segment on the news about these individuals who just wake up and have shown signs of either twitching their fingers, blinking their eyes, or calling out someone's name. Is that not absolutely remarkable?

I remember that, after I experienced a miscarriage, I was totally devastated. These moments of despair usually happened in the earlier part of the morning. Speaking about the loss of this angelic soul was extremely painful for me to do. It was also an arduous task for my husband to do the same. So we developed a language that was only familiar to us. We spoke through the art of touch.

He would hold my hand, and I would place my hands in his. This happened each morning, which stretched out to weeks, then months, and then years. And when this would happen, it was as if my entire soul had been awakened by this gentle touch generated out of love and concern. Today the art of touch is not used for the sole purpose of the miscarriage but for any situation that may be applied to our lives. He could be holding my hand to give support, to express moments of our love, or to display our affection for one another.

Up to this very day, I believe with all my heart and soul that his gentle touch awakened my soul and helped me heal.

Rich thoughts

How has your *touch* awakened others?

_____

_____

_____

_____

_____

_____

_____

_____

_____

_____

_____

_____

_____

Rich Point for Your Day

Today I will become more aware of the touches I receive and the touches I give and will resonate and focus on the power of LOVE.

Life is RICH when you are able to acknowledge that . . .

Determination is a flow of spontaneous thoughts.

Sometimes it feels as if the thoughts that are flowing through my mind are constantly colliding with one another every single second of the day. It truly is amazing that one can conjure up so many creative thoughts in such a short time frame. For me, my thoughts normally run wild when I get lost in the magnificent splendid beauty of nature. That is why I usually surround myself with different writing utensils and apparatuses at all times, for I never know when I will see or hear something that will inspire me so much that all I may want to do is record these moments called life.

My father reminded me that, as long as he can remember, I have been "doing this writing thing" from the time I was a young child. For when I am listening to a song, watching a movie, or even reading a book, that is when the creative juices usually begun to flow, and these were the times when I would make the most connections not only to myself but with others and the world.

For me the summer of 2014 was the most pivotal time for *my* flow of spontaneous thoughts to take flight to that other level! Having had the opportunity to be under one roof filled with women that came from all walks of life and having the opportunity to listen to how their dreams became a reality were not only positive and inspiring but were rather uplifting experiences to be submerged into an environment as such.

Because of the connections that were made at this networking event, it began to propel me further into more of a reflective mode and direction that required me to step out of my comfort zone and make my dreams into a reality.

The determination to believe that all is possible became less challenging for me when I became more focused with my thoughts and visions for the future. This is when the business of Rich Chicks, the programs, the apparel, and the business networking opportunities really came into fruition.

The message that I received from this inspirational event became such a part of my being, and it became very important to me to not allow my eyes to be taken off the prize! And I have not taken my eyes off the prize as yet, for my determination is constantly fed with spontaneity to achieve and succeed in anything that I do, and therefore this continues to propel me forward.

Rich thoughts

Close your eyes and see determination. What does it look like?

_____

_____

_____

_____

_____

_____

_____

_____

_____

_____

_____

Rich Point for Your Day

Today I will be determined to act upon these spontaneous thoughts, transfer them into words, and transform them into action.

Life is RICH when you are able to acknowledge that . . .

You have found the key that unlocks your inward treasures

I remember when I purchased my first property and when I received the key to the front door. It was the most exhilarating feeling I had ever felt. It was somewhat similar to discovering an inward treasure or talent that you were fully unaware of. I jumped around with joy, mapped out what the decor the home would have, and planned for different events that I wanted to host at my new home. However, as time passed that excitement faded away and although it was still a joy, it now just became a slight distance of the past. I was no longer a new homeowner.

The changes that one encounters at a given point in their life are quite similar to that experience I have just mentioned. For when in the midst of one's journey, at some point something has caused one's inward treasures to become buried, hence sadly forgotten.

What many people fail to comprehend is that just as there is a key that is used to enter into your home, everyone also has a key that can open a world of possibilities. For the key is a small-shaped metal with incisions that have been made and cut to fit the wards of a particular lock, and it is usually inserted into a lock so that it can turn to either open or close something.

That exact key can also be used to open or close our God-given talents—our inward treasures. For this key now can provide some sort of means to gaining access to our understanding something that is beyond or greatest dreams.

It may take minutes, hours, days, weeks, months, or even decades; however, what one must never forget is that we all have talents to be used. It is just for us to listen to our inner voices of delight and tap into these gifts in order to really put forth the goodness of these inward treasures.

For when we realize the truth of our God-given purpose, we are able to do a service not only to ourselves but also to others. What an amazing gift that will be!

Rich thoughts

Have you locked or unlocked your inward treasures?

_____

_____

_____

_____

_____

_____

_____

_____

_____

_____

_____

_____

_____

Rich Point for Your Day

Today I will search for that special key. In doing so, I too may unlock my inward treasures.

Life is RICH when you are able to acknowledge that . . .

In the midst of your chaos you can continue to stand.

Sometimes you will stumble and then fall; sometimes you may even fall flat on your face, perhaps in front of crowds of people, for that matter. However, when that does happen, you always find yourself getting back up again. It may be with the assistance of others, or perhaps you have even willed yourself to get back on your own two feet without the help of others. Whether it was with the assistance of another helping hand or by the mere fact that you were able to get up all by yourself, the fact remains that you were able to reach that goal of standing on your own two feet.

You might have found it very hard to stand after having fallen so many times. Perhaps you have studied for a particular exam, only to find out that you did not do as well as you had expected and now sit with a failing grade. Or maybe you are going through various chemotherapy treatments and you are not responding as fast as you would have hoped for, or maybe you have just recently learned that a loved one has died and is no longer here in the physical realm with you.

All these illustrations clearly point to you falling, although not literally on the ground but falling down emotionally, spiritually, and mentally. I too have fallen and have also gotten up, and I sometimes fell again. However, the most important thing to remember is that, in the midst of your chaos, you do have the option to stand. It may be hard, and you may not want to do it today or even want to stand for that matter. I have gone down this road all but too many a times. But keep the door ajar and let the people that love you and who want to help you stand do their part. And keep in mind that just as how a baby learns to crawl, walk, then stand, you too can approach your chaos in the same manner and STAND.

Rich thoughts

When have you taken a stand?

_____

_____

_____

_____

_____

_____

_____

_____

_____

_____

_____

_____

Rich Point for Your Day

Today I will stand by first crawling, walking, and then standing in the midst of my chaos.

Life is RICH when you are able to acknowledge that . . .

Flirting with yourself is sexy.

I was getting ready for Easter Sunday church service and decided to ask my five-year-old nephew who had slept over for the weekend at that time the question "How do I look?" To my surprise, the words that were uttered from this babe's mouth sent me into a whirlwind. His response was "Auntie, you look beautiful and are always beautiful to me!"

It is amazing how powerful words are. And my reaction was a smile that quickly became implanted onto my face, and I thought that, when you think about it, the words that can be uttered out of one's mouth can either build up an individual and bring life to a situation or bring you down and allow you to doubt everything and everyone. And those words from my nephew elevated me to a much higher heights in the realm of self and allowed the love for myself to be that much greater!

Behaving in an alluring way does not always have to be trifling. Being seductive with oneself is a good thing and quite sexy. You may do so with yourself verbally or through written communication as well as through body language, which I recommend to everyone to participate in. Use some Post-it notes and post them sporadically wherever you deem fit. It could be on the bathroom mirror, on your window pane, on your living room wall, on the fridge, or even on the dashboard in your vehicle. If you have not already done so, start acknowledging your beauty and adorn yourself with positive and beautiful affirmations and pour them into your soul at all times. Stand in front of your mirror naked and find positive things to speak as it relates to your once-thought imperfections. Put on your highest stilettos and work them to your benefit because you deserve it!

After I heard those words spoken to me from my nephew, I felt as if I were walking on sunshine and began reconnecting with the actual relationship with myself, and it felt awesome and I felt sexy at the same time. I chose to smother myself in goodness. I began to put more pep into my step, and I found that I began flicking my hair a little bit more and made more eye contact with that sexy person that I observed in the mirror. I was standing a bit taller, and as I continued gazing into the mirror, I found myself titling my head and giving myself a little smile. That is when I reintroduced myself to this feeling of sexiness for self and realized how much fun and more importantly how sexy it is to flirt with oneself.

So thanks to my little nephew, I have rekindled the act of getting my sexy on—again.

Rich Thoughts

List some of the ways that you get your sexy on with yourself.

_____
_____
_____
_____
_____
_____
_____
_____
_____
_____
_____
_____
_____
_____

Rich Point for Your Day

Today I will flirt with myself and enjoy every waking moment of it.

Life is RICH when you are able to acknowledge that . . .

Your breath is your sound track and your kisses are your lullabies.

I absolutely love listening to all genres of music. It could be pop, classical, reggae, gospel, rock, alternative rock, calypso, or jazz. There is something about the relationship between the notes, tempos, and rhythmic sounds that allows my breath to connect with each and every beat. For just as there is something grand about how music is composed and then delivered, there is also something very magical about the love that a parent has for their child, and because of this admiration, this deep-seated relationship dosed in love, hugs, and kisses was also composed for my child.

Listening to the cadenced breath of my son while he sleeps is the most beautiful recording that any musical accompaniment could compose. Sometimes it was a slow breath and other times it was a fast breath. Whatever pattern it was, I loved to hear it because it made me feel relaxed and it sometimes even put me to sleep. But most of all, listening to my son's breath made me feel very special and proud to be his mother because I had the opportunity to share these candid moments with my son.

The kisses that I place upon his forehead and plant upon his cheeks are the quiet yet gentle songs of a mother's love, of my sound track of love that emphasizes the undying, eternal love I continue to sing for and to my son.

I continue to play these lullabies even into his adult life and provide all the rhythmic sounds and pertinent notes of love, kindness, patience, and courage in order to continue teaching my son and providing him with the components of a love sound track.

Rich Thoughts

Give a title of the songs within your sound track of breath.

_____
_____
_____
_____
_____
_____
_____
_____
_____
_____
_____
_____
_____

Rich Point for Your Day

Today I will breathe life into every situation that has tried to prevent me from moving forward.

Life is RICH when you are able to acknowledge that . . .

This too shall pass.

Whenever my friend would encounter or have to battle something in her life, she would always combat the issue—whether it was miniscule or insurmountable—with these few but powerful words: this too shall pass. I was always amazed to see how faithful she was to *just* believe despite any given situation that presented itself to her.

At first I was clueless as to why she has always responded with this phrase, but as the saying goes, practice makes purpose. And so whatever she encountered during those storms prepared her to have faith and allowed her to gather such an unremarkable amount of strength that not only nurtured her will but also propelled her forward in facing her fears.

I used her as an example, and I found myself no longer complaining when having to walk in the valley. So I kept on walking and did not entertain anything. Instead I embraced those moments and also began to utter that this too shall pass. I found that by merely uttering the words "This too shall pass" provided me with an invaluable lesson that the Lord is my Shepherd, and I lack NOTHING. My problems were no longer a problem to me because I chose to realize that I was no longer in control of my present situation. HE was and HE continues to take care of me and will protect me from the things that I am unaware of. And just as how there is calm after the storm, my problems had been dealt with in the same manner. It is easier said than done when you have to trudge down that unexpected path of the unknown, to grumble and complain. However, there comes a point in time when you pull yourself up by the bootstraps and acknowledge the things that are blocking your path or your vision to properly see that they are just that, stumbling blocks designed for that purpose. Only after you have caught on to this will you be able to make each life lesson just that—a life lesson—and to always remember that this too shall pass.

Rich Thoughts

What do you hope for to pass?

_____
_____
_____
_____
_____
_____
_____
_____

_____
_____
_____
_____
_____

Rich Point for Your Day

Today I will not focus on what has been presented to me; I will focus on the things that I have yet to see.

Life is RICH when you are able to acknowledge that . . .

IGNORANCE and STUPIDITY breed more ignorance and stupidity.

The word *ignorant* can best be delineated as something untaught or having to deal with a person who is unaware of something.

I am sure that you have heard people say, "That's so ignorant!" or "He/she is ignorant." Perhaps you have even uttered these words in response to what someone has said or done.

Lately I have been really ignorant about my own needs. I know better and am very familiar with the phrase "Treat others as you would want to be treated." But for some unknown reason, my lack of insight toward myself, sad to say, has not really been a priority for me. Therefore I guess it is safe to say that to a certain extent, I too have fallen short of not knowing what to do when it comes to myself and have therefore have been added to and classed in this category of ignorance.

I find the whole thing to be quite stupid when you really think about it, because I will tell others to take care of themselves in every way that they can. Yet to apply those ideas and thoughts to my own self becomes foreign to me. Don't get me wrong, I love myself, but I find that I expect so much more from myself. Especially when I don't attain the goals that I thought I would have, I get really frustrated.

Even though the things that I do and my profession do not define who I am, these accolades that have been attached to my person for decades speak otherwise to others. I have a bachelor of arts, bachelor of education, and a master's in education, and I am an educator—all completed in my midtwenties. I have always been a perfectionist and have done well. However, what people tend to forget or never see is the hard work that is required in order for these things to get done.

Throughout my childhood, teenage, and adult years, my parents never ever emphasized the need for me to be the best, for their mantra was "As long as you have tried, that is all we can ask for." And so that is what I did, and I was great at it. So the need to give it my all has always been a part of me, which by any means is not a negative thing. But what happens when you no longer know how to give it your all, especially to yourself? This was my most recent dilemma.

People have said that I am extremely hard on myself, and I began to question myself for those stupid wrongdoings. I was so used to being in control of myself and everything else around me that, when I could no longer do all the things that I once was able to do, it became unfamiliar and scary to me. This was foolish in my eyes because I no longer knew how to take care of me, and I felt stupid for not knowing how. These feelings lasted for quite some time, but upon the realization that I had suffered a very traumatic event and what I was feeling was a normal experience, I began to become familiar with myself once more and no longer felt the need to be entertained by the ruthless acts of stupidity or ignorance.

Rich Thoughts

When have you displayed the act of ignorance?

_____

_____

_____

_____

_____

_____

_____

_____

_____

_____

_____

Rich Point for Your Day

Today I will not fall victim to ignorance and stupidity. I will be informed.

Life is RICH when you are able to acknowledge that . . .

Loosening the boundaries of your EGO is not a bad thing at all.

Sometimes your best friend can be your worst enemy—the enemy of self, that is. And when I refer to *ego,* I am not speaking to one's positive attributes. I am referring to that particular person's self-pride—or "I-ness," if you will.

Our ego can be best delineated as our self-image, a person's sense of self-esteem or self-importance that may be characterized by many influencing factors. Some of these factors that mold our egos are done with the help of our family members, loved ones, and even our friends. Other times, our ego may be influenced by external factors, like our place of employment, country of origin, or even religious belief. I always had a healthy ego. Well, so I thought. However, with time, I learned that my ego was quite damaging to my true self and covered up many things.

Fighting with myself, trying to convince my ego that I am not that person who is fearful or doubtful about whether or not I am capable, has done its share in plaguing me.

Interestingly enough, I allowed this to keep myself a hostage, which in turn prevented me from loosening myself from the boundaries of the enemy of self. I have always been expected to do well, because I always had. So when I could not make sense as to what was happening with me, when others would ask how I was doing today, I would respond I am well because of the fact that I believed in words being powerful. Therefore, I spoke wellness and positivity into my life despite what I was feeling and what I was experiencing. After a year or so, I realized that my ego, my *false self,* was not being true to myself. I was not well, and by not acknowledging my anxieties, I became obsessed with covering up the painful thoughts and memories associated with my motor vehicle accident because I wanted to protect my loved ones and the mere fact that I have always done things well. However, I quickly learned that, in order for one to experience light, I also had to know about the dark side and that, once the boundaries of my ego were loosened, it was not a bad thing at all. For the ideal ego is the inner image of oneself as one, and with time that is what I became.

Rich Thoughts

Is having a big ego a negative thing to have?

_____

_____

_____

_____

_____

_____

_____

_____

_____

_____

_____

_____

Rich Point for Your Day

Today I will loosen the boundaries of my ego.

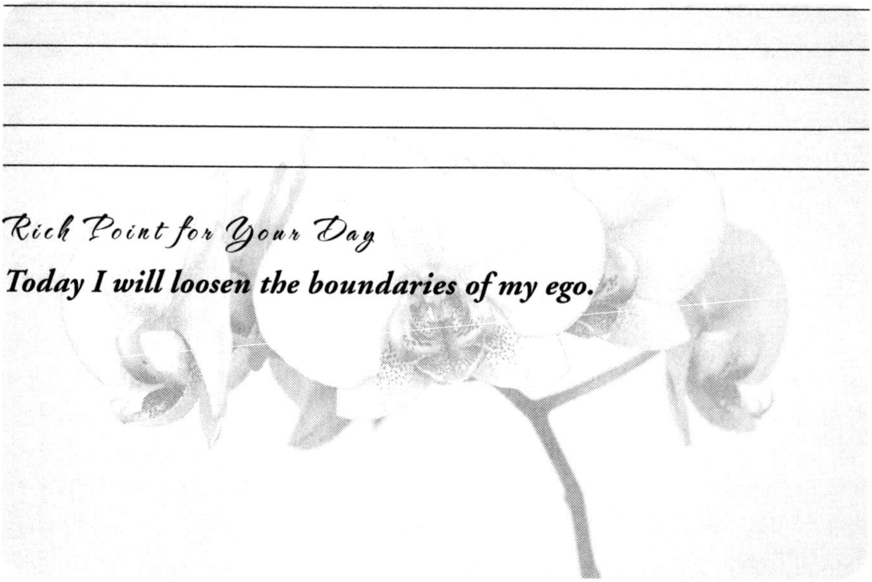

Life is RICH when you are able to acknowledge that . . .

Yesterday's pent-up tears will flow, heal, and educate you more each day.

Crying is a perfectly natural, healthy thing to do. We usually cry in response to strong emotions either during times of sadness, joy, despair, or even anger, despite the fact that it has been classified as the thing that girls, females, or women do, while boys, males, or men are encouraged not to partake in it. I have always been the kind of woman who would shed the few tears. Having said that, I feel no remorse in saying that, in a movie theater, for example, depending on whether or not the story line really captivated my heart, it seems to me that a breathtaking story line always had that effect on me. I have also wept after learning about something exhilarating. I have sobbed when I was driven into total despair after learning that our baby—who my husband and I both had yearned for and whose heartbeat we had listened to on the fetal monitor just the week before—would be miscarried. The loss of my unborn child spiraled me into a place of complete hopelessness, and I cried me a river of anger, frustration, and sadness that left me utterly numb.

However, in the midst of these tears, I later learned that they encouraged healing, and because of the fact that I was able to cry, I had gained remarkable strength and the ability to make the required steps to fully heal. These tears prepared me to equip other women and their families with the required tools to heal and educate themselves in the format of using workshops and programs. My story propelled women forward in the direction of better understanding their health and wellness after experiencing a traumatic event.

In doing so, these women and their families were able to ultimately reflect upon the importance of being refreshed, renewed, and restored because I was most willing to share *my* journey. However, there was a time when I was not always willing to share *my* journey. For *my* steps had led me to a place where I chose not to share for the longest while, which allowed my dialogue to become silenced. However, I realized that crying is quite a positive thing and should never be looked upon as being something negative. Everyone should be made aware that to suppress one's emotions can be unhealthy not only for yourself but for your loved ones as well, and doing so may lead to a plethora of psychological issues.

I became that unhealthy person because of yesterday's pent-up tears and not allowing them to flow freely. And because of this, I did not realize the strong hold that these emotions had on myself. It was only when I had been diagnosed with posttraumatic stress disorder did my steps allow some sort of dialogue. This is where the healing had begun. It was only through those fears and the help of my God, my family, and the counseling that I received that truly allowed me to complete those steps and get back on the right path to educate myself and others on how important it is to rid yourself of yesterday's pent-up tears.

Rich Thoughts

Do you believe that by holding in your tears creates more harm than good?

_____

_____

_____

_____

_____

_____

_____

_____

_____

_____

_____

Rich Point for Your Day

Today my pent-up tears will be released.

.

Life is RICH when you are able to acknowledge that . . .

Dancing with your obstacles allows you to match the speed and rhythm of life with clarity.

I have always loved everything that revolves around the artistic expression of *dance*. I remember that, as a child, many times, I would put my father's dress shoes on, create a dance routine, perform it, and then pretend that I had an audience and that I was a tap dancer. Other times I would unravel the ribbons in my hair and then place them in my hands and turn them around and pretend that I was a renowned ballerina showcasing my artistry. As I got older, the love of dance continued to pump through my veins. I began listening to a variety of music, hearing the beats, and then I would visualize the dance movements. These artistic expressions of dance were then transferred into a story and usually showcased for others to see.

The dancers become the authors, and their dance then depicts a story narrated with the use of the melodic beats and rhythmic sounds of the music. Their voices had been translated into music then become entwined with dancing bodies that told a story that many have lived to tell.

If you have had the opportunity to witness any form of dance performance, you will know that the dancers' clothing, body chemistry, and movement can either captivate the audience's attention or have them uninvolved, depending whether or not they are able to dance through the "obstacles" they may encounter. For it is important that these obstacles are met so that the dancers may continue on until they meet their purpose. In doing so, the dancer advances to the next level of clarity and precision that is acceptable to the both of them—the dancer and the audience.

Just as how dancers have to practice and perfect their dance moves, we also have to practice and aim for purpose in regards to our every move in all areas of our lives. I have had my share of obstacles, and I honestly believe that, because I had the opportunity to stare these obstacles in the face and then dance with them at my own pace, it helped me even more to reflect upon the rhythm of life with a better understanding of this thing called and known to others as life.

It may be difficult, however, to be levelheaded at all times and to make sure that you are aware of your posture, and understanding by taking note of when to dance fast or slow to the melodic beats and rhythmic sounds of the music, keep in mind, is a continuous work in progress. However, please know that the rhythm of life will pan out itself and the flow will become much easier with time. Just continue to believe that you can, and you will do it once you have approached these obstacles while you have danced with truth. Once this is accomplished, the work that is now required of you will be that much more rewarding. For knowing that you were able and determined to adjust the various dance moves to your life, you are most definitely on your way to matching the speed and rhythm of *life* with clarity.

Rich Thoughts

How does dancing relate to avoiding the obstacles we may face in our lives?

_____

_____

_____

_____

_____

_____

_____

_____

_____

_____

_____

_____

_____

Rich Point for Your Day

Today I will dance to the rhythm of the beat like no one is watching and then embrace and celebrate the obstacles in my life.

Life is RICH when you are able to acknowledge that . . .

Love is . . .

Being able to realize that with *love* you are able to believe, hope, and endure all things is by far the most beautiful thing in the world.

In accordance with 1 Corinthians 13: 4–8, it states that love is patient, is kind, and does not envy or behave rudely; love also does not seek its own, provoke others, or allow one to think of evil; but love by far allows one to rejoice in TRUTH.

We all know that love is a beautiful thing that even society has learned to take advantage of. Whether it's Valentine's Day, a birthday, anniversary, graduation, birth, death, promotion, or simply celebrating Mother's Day, Father's Day, or Grandparent's Day for that matter, all these special moments that the world continues to uphold and support on a yearly basis through the purchasing of gifts, which may include chocolates, jewelry, dinners, and sentimental cards, point to how great and powerful our expressions of the love for one another are.

These are the reasons as to why *love* has been deemed the greatest gift of all.

But the reality of things is that each day we are not all going to be loved or feel loved, so what happens when you believe that the greatest gift of all has failed us and has ceased to provide you with the knowledge and experience attached to this natural phenomenon that so many crave for? What happens when this love slowly fades away? Can it or can it not be salvageable?

My family has always been my main priority, extended and immediate, end of story. I remember every one of my first loves—and how could I ever forget them?—my parents, my brother, my first pet, my teachers, my grandparents, and especially my son, my husband, and my life.

However, with the wears and tears of life, especially after the motor vehicle accident, these things began to take their toll on my relationships, and I did not like this feeling, not one bit, especially the path that the relationship with my son and my husband was heading. We became so busy with our lives to the point we had became despondent to the things that we once had loved and practiced on a daily basis.

In order for these voids not to manifest into something bigger, we got back to the basics of doing everything with love. We had to relearn how to be patient with one another and made it a habit to be kind with not only our words but also our actions and even our thoughts. And I, but of course, relearned how to not provoke my son or my husband for the little things that at times seemed bothersome to me. And when we were able to do that, everything ranging from our beliefs, hopes, and desires became enveloped in love once more.

Rich Thoughts

Do you agree that *love* is patient and *love* is kind? Explain why or why not.

_____

_____

_____

_____

_____

_____

_____

_____

_____

_____

_____

_____

Rich Point for Your Day

Today I will remember that, without love, there is no life.

Life is RICH when you are able to acknowledge that . . .

Words are power. So speak positivity into your day.

One could say that negative thoughts and words of lack and limitation create a void mentally and often become impediments to one's positive progression. Many would concur that this screams truth to whether or not you attract negative or positive experiences into your life.

I find that many people do not realize the power that they have just by what is uttered from their mouths.

I would normally tell others to be mindful of their words, thoughts, and actions, yet when it came to me having to do it, I found it difficult to do. It became a chore for me, and I became rather irresponsible when having to pay attention to the importance of the magnitude of my very own words, especially those that I was speaking out into the universe. I would say that I was tired of feeling tired, or that my mind was not working up to par, or that I was fearful.

While I knew better to even think of these things, I became unconscious to the detrimental damage that was being harvested over my life. That is when I decided to actually walk the walk and be more conscious of my words. I began using words that were positive or progressive. This required some time on my part and, believe it or not, mustered up a whole lot of discipline to do so.

Being able to "program" your mind and having to abstain from the old forms of negative thinking and then actually replacing them with a brand-new positive thinking will continuously be a work in progress.

However, when I think of this simple phrase "Words are power," this new process of replacing positive thoughts of love and abundance becomes less of a chore and allows thoughts to be expressed more freely through me.

Rich Thoughts

What kind of words is uttered from your mouth?

_____

_____

_____

_____

_____

_____

_____

_____

_____

_____

_____

_____

_____

_____

Rich Point for Your Day

Today I choose to be mindful of my words for there is power that can ultimately speak life and positivity or death and destruction.

Life is RICH when you are able to acknowledge that . . .

Life is like a classroom.

As far as I can remember, I have always loved school. At the tender age of ten, I used to "play school" with my brother. I as the teacher and he as the student had allowed me to create and mark many meaningful assignments and of course discipline him when needed. I also remember not being able to sleep the night before the first day back to school. I would become so excited, just thinking about the opportunity I would have of getting to see all my friends whom I was unable to touch base with during the summer. I also became really excited because now I was finally going to be able to use all my new school stuff and meet my new teachers for the upcoming academic school year. But more importantly, I believe that I looked forward to learning more fascinating things than I did in the previous academic school year.

It is quite funny when you think about it that my love for learning still continued in pretty much my teenage, youth, and adult years. Upon completion of my bachelor of arts, I chose to rightfully enter into the realm of education as an educator. Amusingly enough, the excitement and anticipation for the first day of school commenced when I first became a student and then as an educator and was sustained throughout my entire teaching profession. These feelings became part of me because of my desire to continue learning. As an educator, learning happened twice—first as I prepared for my students, then as I learned from them. If I were to compare one's life to a classroom, the commonality of the two would be that whatever you are assigned in life within the classroom, you will *never* stop learning.

As a teacher you are forever and a day preparing yourself and your students for success. From an educator's point of view, you get yourself ready by preparing yourself for your lessons by either attending professional development workshops, reading, researching, or partnering with other teachers. As students, they prepare themselves for class by either having all the required materials should there be a test or should they have to complete an assignment of some sort. The students have to make sure that all the expectations were made to their best ability.

Life is somewhat like a class in the sense that, in order to receive optimal results, a lot of time, effort, and dedication will be needed. There will be times when those life assignments, projects, tests, and exams will not produce 100 percent. However, just as how a teacher would reflect upon the various kinds of modifications that could be implemented on a daily basis so that their students meet, pass, and surpass the success criteria for the various academic subject areas, human beings also adapt the similar survival traits to their lives.

Just as teachers continuously reflect upon how they can become better, we must also do the same for ourselves and with the various tests of life. We have to prepare for the daily tests of life. We must also realize and fully understand that, should we fail on one of our life test, we should not give up or be discouraged. We should understand that life will forever be our classroom. It is just how we equip ourselves with the tools given to us by taking these tests that will ultimately allow us to pass or fail.

Rich Thoughts

When have you had to take on the role of a teacher or a student in your lifetime?

_____

_____

_____

_____

_____

_____

_____

_____

_____

_____

_____

_____

Rich Point for Your Day

Today I will become both the student and teacher, for each day is a test that I will either receive a passing or failing grade.

Life is RICH when you are able to acknowledge that . . .

Walls eventually crumble.

Yes, of course. There is the azure sky that accompanies this magnificent body of crystal clear water, and how could I forget the white sand that seems endless to the naked eye? Or what about participating in jet skiing and having the ability to tour part of the island in a glass-bottom boat? Or perhaps you have just opted to simply lie on the beach, on your beach towel, in order to get ready to be kissed by the sun. All these activities are enticing and really great to do, but I failed to mention another beach activity that so many sun worshippers love to do—creating sand castles!

This particular beach treasure often requires a lot of time and energy due to Mother Nature herself. I would always create sand castles when I visit the beach, and quite super focused, if I may add. Whatever I had visualized in my mind becomes transformed into *my* reality—of course with the help of the tons of sand ready at my disposal on the beach. The only problem is that, no matter where you set up shop for the creation of this sand castle, 80 percent of the time, the waves tend to carry the sand back into the depths of the sea even if you are quite far from the shoreline. Usually when this happens, the sand castle walls begin to crumble, and you can get frustrated that the sand castle's foundation is no longer the structure that you want and watch the sand crumble. Or you can attempt to build up the pieces again that have become broken and have collapsed during the process. I usually chose to rebuild my sand castle rather than watch my creative sand masterpiece gradually disintegrate into nothing.

Having the walls in your life can also crumble; however, just like the sand castles, they too can also be rebuilt. And while others may think that, when walls crumble, it is an awful thing, I beg to differ because a crumbling wall can be a pleasant thing. Not only can the walls save a person but perhaps this crumbling foundation is symbolic to your life and is the only way that your life can be restored.

So when you are reluctant to restore your walls, remember that a broken wall is a thing of beauty for a certain time. You must also realize that something's in life do not last forever and requires change, and therefore it must crumble in order to remain strong.

Rich Thoughts

What walls need to be broken down?

_____
_____
_____
_____
_____
_____
_____
_____
_____
_____
_____
_____

Rich Point for Your Day

Today I will rebuild the walls that have crumbled in my life and remain optimistic.

Life is RICH when you are able to acknowledge that . . .

When we sail in the ocean, we might occasionally drift.

High winds and rains have always been somewhat of a challenge for those having to travel during the stormy season. Rather than dreading what could possibly turn out to be a natural disaster, these large vessels continue to be navigated through the storms. These high winds allow the sail to be harnessed for a speedy navigation despite the fact that they may occasionally drift from the crashing waves.

Navigating these large vessels in the ocean is quite similar to the storms that come our way. Stormy circumstances are inevitable, and at times we don't know what to do when these "natural" disasters present themselves within our lives. Although our first reaction may be to run from these storms, we can instead learn how to receive help so that we may use these tools to navigate through them all.

These storms do have to stop, and when they have taken a different path, we are brought out of our distresses. This is just like the many stories that we have recently heard of in relation to the cruise ships being stranded out at sea and leaving the vacationers in a not-so-happy and sometimes life-compromising state.

They too were in a great deal of frustration and distress and experienced an enormous amount of fear; however, upon arrival of the safety crew, these people who were left stranded for days became hopeful and were rescued.

Many of them spoke of how dissatisfied they were with the services and that they would have to think about if they would ever go on another cruise ever again. While others spoke to the media about how they remained optimistic during this time of uncertainty, others spoke about turning their negative experience into something memorable.

Just as some of the vacationers realized that they were in trouble and rode it out, so to speak, we must also know that, when we sail in the ocean, we might occasional drift, but it is okay to do so. For this is when we are able to use our storms as an opportunity to exercise the notion that all will be well and that we will be delivered and more importantly will be granted the peace we all deserve!

Rich Thoughts

Have you ever drifted away from an original plan?

_____

_____

_____

_____

_____

_____

_____

_____

_____

_____

_____

_____

_____

Rich Point for Your Day

Today I will see where the sail of my ship navigates me.

Life is RICH when you are able to acknowledge that . . .

You exemplify strength.

It must have been a year ago when my mother had told me how much she admires me. They were the most humbling words I ever heard. These words uttered from my mother's mouth had evoked a wealth of emotions, for I always have admired my parents, both my father and mother. However, this particular conversation with my mother allowed me to reflect upon the many reasons as to why I love and admire her so much.

It isn't just because of her beauty, sassiness, intelligence, and undying love for her family that makes me love this woman; it is her strength she carries forward in each of her roles as a daughter, sister, mother, grandmother, aunt, friend, and wife.

Today was no different from any other day. For at times my mother and I would speak at least ten times for the day, we usually spoke about issues pertaining to the world, ourselves, or where life has taken us. These are just some of the things we would sometimes speak about. I am not sure how we even came to the discussion pertaining to strength. Perhaps it was because my mother has seen my exhaustion within the past few years. She was right; I was exhausted—drained, to be quite frank with you. So when my mother empathized with me and felt horrible that I had to go through the motions of yuckiness, my mother reassured me that what I was going through would make me even stronger than I already am. She spoke to me about the importance of not giving up and holding my head up high and shared her most intimate experiences of how she persevered during the battles of life. The stories that were shared with me that day left me feeling like I was the only woman left standing and that I could accomplish anything that would come my way—all in the name of one simple yet powerful phrase that was spoken to me out of love: "You are the strongest woman I know."

Thank you, Mommy, for those kind words. They have reminded me that the hardest battles are given to God's strongest soldiers. In doing so, you have reminded me that strength is not always something that is physical. Strength is the persistence to never give up!

Rich Thoughts

When did you have to exercise your strength?

Rich Point for Your Day

Today I will be strong and utter the phrase "I will NEVER give up."

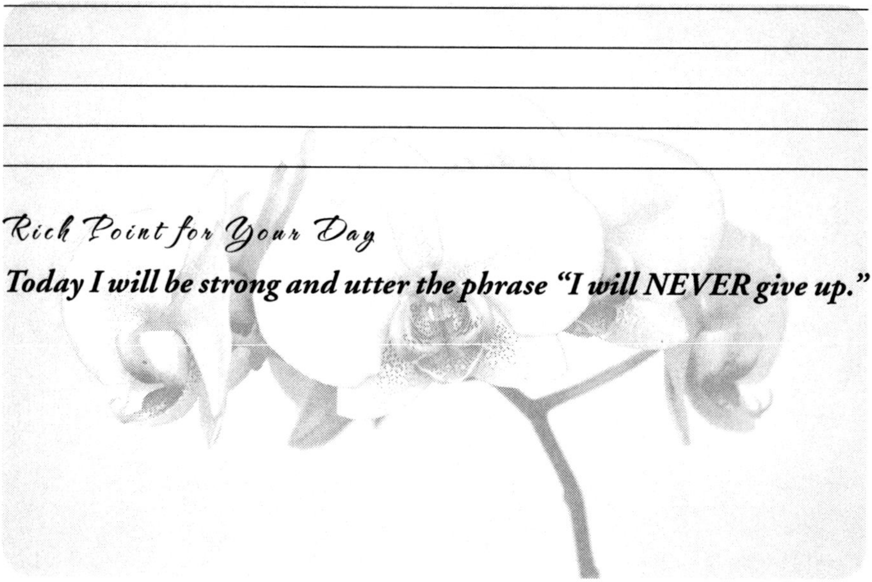

Life is RICH when you are able to acknowledge that . . .

You are your own author.

Literature has so many genres and great authors, each complimenting each other. Whether it is mystery, romance, adventure, fantasy, thriller, horror, historical fiction, nonfiction, and fiction, people take on the role of the characters in the novel that now has become their "new" life.

I absolutely love reading and have always boasted about the fact I am able to visualize all the fine details about the plot, the setting, and the many characters. I think the reason as to why the words that I would read would come to life was because of all the connections I was able to make with myself, the texts, and the world. In doing so, I was able to relate more to each sentence, paragraph, and chapter. Being able to infer and question the motives of the character piqued my interest and allowed suspense to be created.

If a movie was created from a novel, I would chose the novel any day because of the way I would visualize things was by far in greater detail than I could ever imagine any movie ever capturing it. Usually it seemed to be on point, while the other times it seemed as if I saw so much more than what the movie had to offer.

Whether these characters experienced conflicts with their environment, with others, or with themselves or found issues within the greater society, they always seemed to be resolved. Either in a complex, long, or drawn-out kind of way or meticulously adventurous, a book allows the reader or the audience to fully digest the lessons that were taught or that had to be learned.

What if you were your own author? What would the title of your novel be? What genre would you choose, and who would be your target audience? Think of all the components of a novel and reflect upon how your words can affect you and the life you live. How would your novel affect the lives of others? That is definitely the kind of author that I strive to be.

Rich Thoughts

What is your favorite genre to read and why?

_____

_____

_____

_____

_____

_____

_____

_____

_____

_____

_____

_____

Rich Point for Your Day

Today I will write a book titled Surrender and will be opened to the lessons of our life challenges. I will remain eager to learn and grow.

Life is RICH when you are able to acknowledge that . . .

Your once-invisible voice will regain strength.

I remember my grade 5 math teacher and how intense all her classes were. Students were placed in rows, nothing like how the teachers strategically plan the seating of their students nowadays. In her class, there were no math groups, differentiated learning, or even the integration of technology to make the learning of the math concepts fun. I guess that this lack could be attributed to the fact that these classes were a long time ago. Her hair was cut in the fashion of a short bob. She had this long wooden ruler that she would hold in her hand as she circled in on her next prey. If you were not paying attention or did not know the answer to her endless math questions, the long wooden ruler would be hit on the students' desk. This not only got the attention of each and every one of the students, it created an atmosphere of fear and therefore promoted an environment of invisible, silent voices from most of the students except for those who were the classroom pets.

I was one of those students who felt intimidated at times because of her demeanor. Most of the time I would know the answer, but because of my fear of the possibility of not answering the teacher's math question to her liking, I opted to have that *invisible* voice so that I may be spared from any form of embarrassment. Choosing the option that I did was by far the safest route. It was only through my daily after school chats with my parents about my day at school did the issue of my invisible voice in math class come up.

My father spoke to me about not letting anyone ever intimidate me or make me feel any less than I am. His conversation went on to explain the importance of speaking up for oneself and not letting my dialogue ever be compromised or silenced. After that discussion with my father, I had a new source of inner strength that allowed me to shine brighter than any star in the sky. I began reviewing my notes on a constant basis and also began to raise my hand when the math teacher poised her questions to the class. It was only then did I realize that I had given this math teacher the permission to make me feel uncomfortable and question my capability and understanding some of the math concepts, equations, and formulas. Once the secret was let out of the bag, my invisible voice no longer was an issue.

My dialogue was no longer silenced by this math teacher, and because of this realization, I gained enormous confidence, self-esteem, and strength because of the invaluable lessons learned from my dear father.

Rich Thoughts

Have you ever felt invisible or felt as if your dialogue had been silenced?

_____

_____

_____

_____

_____

_____

_____

_____

_____

_____

_____

Rich Point for Your Day

Today I will consciously work at making the invisible visible.

Life is RICH when you are able to acknowledge that . . .

Random acts of kindness are kind acts randomly done.

We now live in a world where people have become so caught up with themselves or too preoccupied with having any caring qualities. The media and the actions of our world has instilled a sense of fear, where the inability to trust others has become the norm. We tend to deliberately turn a blind eye to those in need, which now seems to be the path that everyone takes.

Gone are the days of random acts of kindness. They are definitely a distant memory of the past. That is why I have made the conscious effort to treat others as I would like to be treated, whether it is by giving a gift in the format of a smile, holding the door, giving a complete stranger a compliment, or perhaps donating various things, like time or even money.

I try to give back in any way that I can. Some days it exceeds ten people, while other days it may be only four people. All in all, that willingness to humble myself and allow another individual to shine so that their dreams may also be fulfilled is the most rewarding experience. Therefore, why would I not do anything else but give!

We were in the midst of moving, and while doing so, it dawned on me that our son had a lot of untouched or gently used items, which included plush animals and many children's toys, educational hardcover and softcover children's books, pencils, erasers, and board games. We discussed different options as a family as to what we could do with these excess items. My son decided that it would be kind of cool to donate all his children's toys and books that had gone untouched for years to a nearby Daycare. What a wonderful idea! So the following day I contacted a nearby day care and spoke with a supervisor and asked her if she would be interested in these children's items. She was more than elated to know that we had chosen her day care and more importantly that we thought of the children and wanted to do this. I guess anyone would be taken aback by this phone call, especially during this day and age where everyone is for themselves and never gives anything away for free. The day care supervisor continuously said thank you and spoke about how excited the children were going to be. Furthermore, she said that the items were so much in need. My response was that the pleasure was mine and that I would tell my son these kind words that she expressed to me that fine spring day.

This conversation about this random act of kindness sparked a selfless gesture on our son's part to continue giving to others. Now we make it our duty to give to those we believe may need it, effortlessly, on a monthly basis. What an amazing feeling it is to give without having to receive anything back in return.

Rich Thoughts

Think of a few illustrations of the act of kindness and then list them.

_____
_____
_____
_____
_____
_____
_____
_____
_____
_____
_____
_____
_____
_____

Rich Point for Your Day

Today I will try to select at least five random people so that I may act kindly toward them.

Life is RICH when you are able to acknowledge that . . .

You are your own architect.

We can all be master architectural engineers. However, before that can ever be accomplished, we must possess the ability to be willing to build upon the structure that has already been created. These architects may choose to design these structures with different materials. Some will go as far as to include some gold, silver, and precious stones, while others opt to include perhaps a small percentage of wood, hay, or even straw, for that matter, to their structural designs. The grand reward comes in the format of how well their architectural structure withstands the four seasons and possibly any natural disasters.

Adolescents are also special beings in the sense that they are their own architects. And if they are not careful, just as how structures can either endure the natural elements or suffer loss, adolescents may experience the same as well.

Being an adolescent in today's society can be really, really hard if you are not adequately equipped with the necessary tools required in "making it." It's like this generation can no longer have fun or be a child, for they are faced with so many adult issues that have been forced on them. As a result they are caught in a tug of war between the two and end up losing their innocence much earlier than our generation ever did.

If you are ever in doubt of all the negative things that have been dosed on our youths within our community, just tune in to one of the many news channels, then you will quickly understand what I am talking about.

I never understood why more youth and young adolescent programs have not been a priority for the politicians and wider community. These programs should be placed in all the neighborhoods in and around the city. I truly believe, by implementing these programs, a lot of the problematic issues youth and young adults are currently facing and will continue to face would be at least moved beyond the dialogue stage, and these detrimental stages in our youths' lives would be seriously tackled and addressed, and then perhaps a solution that may actually be implemented may be worked on. We talk a good talk, but when it comes to walking the walking, well, there needs to be more of that.

It is a given fact that both our young females and males need outlets to express themselves, but more importantly they need to be heard. Sometimes it just takes that one individual to show a vested interest in another in order for great results to manifest. In a sense these youths and young adults need to believe to succeed. This is where inspiration comes into play, for if they are to have someone who can assist them to plan and model a template for success, they will embark on their journey toward becoming an *architect* and *become* more proficient within our society and the wider community at large. It would also be amazing if the adults who are assisting the future generation become architects too. In doing so, we would all work together to empower each other not only to take control of our lives but to construct knowledge, skills, and values within the context and awareness of self.

Rich Thoughts

Have you ever built anything before? How successful were you and why do you think you were?

_____

_____

_____

_____

_____

_____

_____

_____

_____

_____

_____

_____

Rich Point for Your Day

Today I will plan and model a template for success, enabling them to be leaders, not followers; in control, not out of control; powerful, not powerless.

Life is RICH when you are able to acknowledge that . . .

MIRACLES come in many forms.

I was speechless. All I wanted to do was to open the blinds to let in some of that morning radiant sunshine in to my parents' condo. I had dropped by for a brief minute just to say hello. Instead I was greeted by such an enormous creature that turned its head and glared at me as if I were interrupting its morning. I could not believe what I saw, for first and foremost, it was quite rare to be able to see a bird of prey in the heart of the city—this was absolutely unheard of.

I motioned for my mother to make her way toward to where I was standing. She was also surprised to see such a sight. It was a peregrine falcon, and we were hearing a lot about this bird lately. Why it decided to perch on the railing of the balcony that morning, I do not know. However, that was not the only time that we received a visit from our feathered friend.

I quickly and most quietly got my camera and began to take its picture. Once again I was astonished by the human characteristics this bird had displayed. He slowly turned his head around, looked at me, and basically posed for the picture. The falcon remained there for some time, and when it had enough, it spread its wings, which must have had a wingspan of at least eight feet. Then this beautiful creature flew off.

When I think about that morning, I am still in disbelief and consider this visit from this bird to be a miracle in a different form. A miracle in the sense that this visit was a huge surprise and quite rare. Therefore, I was convinced that it lead to be the work of divinity.

I began researching about this bird and found out that it had migrated from the United States and had taken up residency in Toronto for a few years; furthermore, it had been sighted in the various parts of our city. As I began researching more about the *symbolic* meaning of peregrine falcons, I learned that they represent superiority, spirit, light, freedom, and aspiration.

All in all, I do not think that this falcon just happened to visit my parents' dwelling and sit comfortably perched on the balcony railing— not once but twice in the span of a week. I believe that its visit meant something. For I remember having sighted this falcon again three times for the year. And then again when my family and I moved into another home, I sighted my friend two more times. And just last week, I am sure that I saw a baby falcon, its offspring, flying in front of our home. This is *not* by chance. This feathered friend continues to symbolize an emblem for success for my family. For it remains to be victorious in the sense that the falcon continues to speak to our ability to persevere and rise above any situation that may have presented itself to us or that have tried to stifle us. And because of the strong connection we hold dear to our heart, this is our living testimony that WE will always rise above the occasion and soar high in the sky like our feathered friend, the falcon.

Rich Thoughts

What miracle have you hoped for?

_____

_____

_____

_____

_____

_____

_____

_____

_____

_____

_____

_____

_____

Rich Point for Your Day

Today I am reminded that miracles show up when we are least expected.

Life is RICH when you are able to acknowledge that . . .

Faith grows best in the winter of trial.

All our challenges and any sense of limitation or feeling of being alone and unsupported stem from fear. It is only when we are able to align ourselves with our true SELVES will we be able to lift the limitation of what we are able to accomplish to become our reality.

It was the winter of 2010 and the burdens of life were really starting to get to me. Disappointment, confusion, anger, and frustration—these are the emotions that I carried with me on a daily basis.

Mind you, I did not always feel this way, nor did I enjoy the toxic realities; however, having experienced the numerous trials and then having to endure it all over again had triggered a string of other trials, and to say the least, it was becoming less bearable for me, and I began to crumble. My faith was wavering; therefore, I literally wavered too! And when you replace faith with fear, be prepared for the unexpected trials and tribulations of life to set in.

For many, these trials may include the loss of a job, the death of a loved one, an unwanted pregnancy, or even a divorce. However, for me it was everything associated with the losses that happened after my motor vehicle accident—mainly the issues that revolved around my health and more importantly my peace of mind.

What people fail to realize is, in the midst of these life-changing winter trials, as I call them, you find that usually these experiences tend to build one's character and produce an enormous amount of patience.

The winter season may seem for many that all is hopelessly dead, bleak, naked, cold, and dreary. However, it is during this season that I say that faith truly commenced and produced some amazing results. It is during the winter months that the ground begins to surrender to the cold and slowly makes a conscious effort to rise from the earth of death to the earth of transformation.

In the midst of this chaos, winter had symbolized death and stagnation, and loved ones and friends chose to see what they could see, not realizing how misguided they had become about my changes, beauty, strength, and ability to cope.

Yet despite the darkness that was faced during these winter months, this season taught me the importance of faith, hope, and oneness. Perhaps it was the purity and freshness of the first snowfall that did it for me, because when it snowed, all my cares and worries also became covered. Snowstorms represented the trials and tribulations of my journey and reminded me of the steps that I had taken. But more importantly, these steps had produced footprints that reminded me that I was never really ever alone.

They illustrated to me that my Creator has always been there with me, had never forsaken or left me, and would always remain by my side. And because of this, I am most grateful for this winter wonderland.

Rich Thoughts

When have you had to walk by faith and not by sight?

_____

_____

_____

_____

_____

_____

_____

_____

_____

_____

_____

_____

Rich Point for Your Day

Today let faith comfort me when I am in the winter trials.

Life is RICH when you are able to acknowledge that . . .

A family that prays together stays together!

Praying in the morning is part of our daily routine. We pray as a family because we know the importance of giving thanks to our Heavenly Father. In addition to giving thanks and praise, prayer also continues to work at solidifying our family unit.

For when we do pray as a family, it becomes such an instrumental tool that is not only used to equip us but used to strengthen us.

We would normally start our day out with prayer by standing in a circle. We would then hold each other's hands and allow the Holy Spirit to have its way. Sometimes I would start with the prayer, while the other times in the mornings it would be our son who would proceed with prayer; and if not our son, my husband would lead.

To some this may sound strange and feel awkward, and at first you may even stumble a bit with what you would like to say; however, in no time, the words you are searching for would begin to flow like honey.

We would commence with what we are thankful for and what we would like to see happen for our family and friends near and far, and then we would pray for our wider community and world at large. I will admit that, when things became too hectic and the prayers were not being done as they normally would have been, you would see that difference in our lives because of the inconsistencies with our prayers; and the things in our lives also became unbalanced and riddled with confusion.

However, one thing that I can attest to is that there is power in the name of Jesus, and there is power to mend all things that requires fixing. My family and I are living proof of this.

Although many people would think that the requirement for prayer should consist of long, well-thought-out words, these are not a necessity for one to let go and let God carry the heavy load or burden of life for you. Your words can be as simple as "Father God, you know my heart . . ." or you may merely just utter the word *Father*. So don't let the semantics of prayer get in the way. Breathe and pray life into your family and family members.

Rich Thoughts

What prayer have you prayed recently?

_____

_____

_____

_____

_____

_____

_____

_____

_____

_____

_____

_____

_____

Rich Point for Your Day

Today I will bow humbly before you and give thanks for all that you do.

Life is RICH when you are able to acknowledge that . . .

You must remain calm and NEVER forget to breathe.

Research points to human beings being able to live for up to three months without food, three days without water, and approximately three minutes before they perish. We take a lot of things for granted on a daily basis, and breathing is one of them. It deserves so much more attention to what it has been given. Hence there is a recent rise in meditation, mindfulness, and particularly breathing exercises for those who thirst a better understanding of the benefits of breathing, for living in such a society as the one we do can cause an enormous amount of stress. Instead of us approaching anything that comes our way with calmness, our initial response is to panic and hold our breath. I too have found at times it to be rather difficult to breathe during times of distress.

I have also learned from the many mindfulness meditations that breathing is a much more fundamental activity that is quite successful in displacing erratic breathing rates and rhythms especially when in a state of anxiety, anger, or fear. Therefore, the release of the toxins was a bonus, and this promotes better health and wellness for any individual.

Having said that, I decided to follow through with my mother's advice by joining a yoga class. She suggested it initially because of her knowledge of the breath and how it can influence how one feels and also assist with one's pain.

Participating in the yoga class on a weekly basis was a phenomenal experience. My instructor and her regimen allowed me to feel so relaxed during these sessions and stirred up circulation points within my body that were dormant for years. I found that, by being able to control my breathing, there came health results. Being able to lie flat, straight on my back, and having the option to listen to soothing music while the instructor directed us into a land full of tranquility was the best thing for me at that time. For I truly benefited from these breathing exercises by becoming a calmer person than I was before.

Although it may be difficult to relax during times of distress, I am able detect the stressors, acknowledge them, then focus on my breathing to regulate my breath in order to ensure that I remain at one with myself.

Rich Thoughts

When have you used the breathing technique in your life?

_____

_____

_____

_____

_____

_____

_____

_____

_____

_____

_____

_____

_____

_____

Rich Point for Your Day

Today I will let my breath direct me to the path of peace.

Life is RICH when you are able to acknowledge that . . .

Sacrifice promotes believability.

It was not by choice that we had to sit at home with no form of social media, but due to my negligence and habit of procrastination to pay the bill on time, our home television package was disconnected. At first it was like torture wanting to watch *Scandal*, a television show that had me literally sitting at the edge of my seat during each episode. Or the occasional soap opera, movie, the local news, or CNN. However, as the days went by, the realization that our beloved pastime of watching television was no longer regarded as important or even worthy.

Our reality was that our bill had been neglected for some time and now we had to suffer the consequences of having to live and make the sacrifice of watching nil television shows. However, being unable to do so forced us to appreciate the basic necessities of life and allowed us to revert to the things that we enjoyed doing the most—spending some real *family* time together.

During this time, we began reading more as a family, I began writing more and we began doing the traditional family things a little bit more, like eating breakfast and dinner around the dinner table, asking how each other's day went, then actually listening to what each other had said. We laughed and goofed around more and it felt great! Don't get me wrong, we used to do these family things before; however, having more time on our hands, we reverted to the good old days of spending time with one another. It seemed that we had to make the decision to sacrifice all the activities associated with the television, and then the family became more believable in the sense that we were able to achieve getting to know each other through better communication and an understanding for one another because of this quality time we were reintroduced to.

Rich Thoughts

What have you had to give up?

_____

_____

_____

_____

_____

_____

_____

_____

_____

_____

_____

_____

Rich Point for Your Day

Today I will sacrifice something that I normally cannot do without and appreciate my time without it.

Life is RICH when you are able to acknowledge that . . .

Less is more.

Isn't funny that, when we begin to grow up, we start to see and appreciate things differently and realize that the "friendships" that we considered to be of such great importance may not be so important after all.

What allows friends to get to this point where we realize that maybe the friendship has served its purpose, and when do we know if it is the right time to move on? Interestingly enough, I too have fallen victim to this new realization that having more friends does not necessarily mean that it is better. Although at first this was very difficult for me to grasp, with time it made absolute sense to me as to why the friends who were a part of my life for such a long period of time were no longer a part of the *friendship* equation. It was simple. We grew apart, which therefore allowed me to question what makes a friendship real in the first place.

In a world where words are carefully rehearsed, being straightforward can be refreshing. That is one of the most important characteristics of a true friend. For real friends will speak the truth to us in love, even if it isn't what we would want to hear. The friendships that I had were like that. They were never founded on secondary issues but instead were based on being able to speak to one another's deepest issues and needs of the heart.

While we find comfort in the familiarity of those we depend on in life, it is also very important for us to recognize that at times *things* or *people* can be substituted.

Similarly, I found that though the people who comprised those friendships were great friends, with time I too was able to speak candidly to the true conditions of their hearts and realized that less is more. For some people speak and act like they are for you, when in actuality they celebrate your downfall and rejoice when troubled waters begin to flood and attempt to wash away everything that you have ever had. Although difficult to digest, being able to sever all ties with these individuals is required in order for your growth to be that of greatness.

Overall, beyond common interests, beyond affection, wit, and laughter, people must realize that at one point in their lives these gifts also become substituted and more importantly that it is normal for this to happen when you come to the realization that less IS more.

Rich Thoughts

Have you had a friendship that for whatever reason had no longer *felt* the same? How did you feel and how did you confront this friendship issue?

_____

_____

_____

_____

_____

_____

_____

_____

_____

_____

_____

_____

Rich Point for Your Day

Today I will continue to realize that it becomes LESS important to have more friends and MORE important to have REAL ones.

Life is RICH when you are able to acknowledge that . . .

Life is like a roller coaster.

Roller coasters have recently been added to my list of things that are no longer considered to be fun. Perhaps with age also comes truth, and my truth to the life of roller coasters is that I am no longer that teenager who would drop everything that I was doing just to meet up with friends and family to ride every ride in the amusement park. Reality can sometimes be a bummer, especially upon the realization that being frightened to a point of no return and occasionally having to gasp for air as you try to remain calm are no longer cool.

I will never forget the time I was coaxed into joining a never-ending line only to be strapped into a death-defying ride.

Life is a lot like roller coasters at an amusement park. You get in, knowing that you will experience many dips, twists, and turns, and you just don't know how fast these things will occur. And when you experiences these "jolts," you experience yet another ride in itself of going up and then going down.

That may be a fun strategy for roller coasters, but not such a fun strategy for life. For when you experience the ups and downs and twists and turns in life, these actions and reactions only escalate matters. However, what one should understand is that just as how we are able to prepare ourselves for the unknown when we ride these roller coasters, we can also prepare ourselves for the unknowns that we are sometimes faced with on a daily basis in our lives.

Roller coasters don't necessarily have to be a bad thing; it can be a fun experience. Well, perhaps not. But there is one thing that I do know is that we can find alternative ways to deal with these "jolts" in our lives. And although it may have been a terrible ride, we can use those rides to learn how to prepare ourselves for the unseen and the unknown.

Rich Thoughts

When life throws you for a loop, how do you address these malfunctions
you have experienced during your ride of life?

_____
_____
_____
_____
_____
_____
_____
_____
_____
_____
_____
_____

Rich Point for Your Day

**Today I will embrace and celebrate the many dips, twists, and
turns that may take me upside down, right side up. All in all, I will
continue to enjoy the ride.**

Life is RICH when you are able to acknowledge that . . .

Spiritual soil allows one's mind to flourish.

"Children Learn What They Live" is an absolutely remarkable poem that speaks to how precious and impressionable children are. This poem is also very instrumental in reminding us about how important our role as adults is in these precious lives.

When I was a child, this poem became a permanent fixture on my parents' fridge and has now become a tool to equip and inspire my entire household.

The soil is just like a child. If you want to grow flowers, fruits, or vegetables, you better make sure that the soil is up to par and free from anything that will alter the normal growth pattern.

Similarly a child's growth requires the same kind of soil, one that is free from rocks, pebbles, insects, or thorns. For if those things are present, it may alter them in such a way we would not have intended for them to grow. Just like these fruits, children also require to be sown on fertile grounds and be placed within a good environment in order to ensure the best and most promising results. In addition to having the appropriate soil, water is also needed to maintain a healthy and productive life. For when you apply water to these fruits, it allows them to flourish and bear abundantly. Therefore, because as adults we are the decisive elements in our children's lives, we must also be *very* mindful of our approach to our children's lives. The climate that is set within our homes; the daily moods create their climate and determine whether or not their lives will be miserable or joyous. Let us continue to be a tool of inspiration where we allow their minds to spiritually flourish.

Rich Thoughts

What are the steps that you have taken to ensure that the seeds that you have planted remain to grow and prosper spiritually?

_____

_____

_____

_____

_____

_____

_____

_____

_____

_____

_____

_____

Rich Point for Your Day

Today I will be an instrument of inspiration and the soil that allows my child's mind to flourish.

Life is RICH when you are able to acknowledge that . . .

The rain dances with the sky.

I have never ever heard the rain pour in the manner that it did, nor did I ever hear the thunder rumble and roar like that before, nor do I remember the lightning literally lighting up the somber skies the way that it did the other night. I couldn't help but think that Mother Nature was extremely unhappy with her inhabitants.

When the meteorologists predict that there will be rain in the forecast, many people begin to grumble and complain because their outdoor plans have become spoiled. But anyone who has experienced a drought knows that rain is actually a blessing, for it nourishes the earth in many ways and therefore benefits us all.

I on the other hand welcome any type of rain. It could be a downpour of rain, drizzles of rain, or even rain showers. For I continue to see rain as a natural source of strength and far from being the enemy that so many have labeled it to be. So when I see the rain dancing with the sky, I am thankful for the things of this world that have battered me on the outside because the storms that threaten to destroy us really do strengthen us.

So every time that it rains, it has become a beautiful reminder to me that each and every day I am being built up on the inside so that I may continue to stand straight, strong, and sound in the comfort of knowing that my blessings are on their way.

Rich Thoughts

Do you welcome the rain or wish it away? What is the significance or the meaning of rain for you? What does it symbolize?

_____
_____
_____
_____
_____
_____
_____
_____
_____
_____
_____
_____
_____

Rich Point for Your Day

Today I shall remember that rain showers are a time of growth for the things unseen to the naked eye, which will manifest in its rightful form and time.

Life is RICH when you are able to acknowledge that . . .

You cannot see the shadow if you keep your face to the sunshine.

Today was the first day of May and the weather was absolutely beautiful. To say the least, we had quite a winter, and although spring gave us a run for our money, today's balmy temperature had definitely made up for all the other lost times that the weather had failed us.

As I looked out of the window of my home, I could see that more people had chosen to dress less "winterish" today. Many people opted to not wear their coats and made the conscious decision to wear their brightly colored spring jackets or sweaters. Some even chose to wear shorts. However, for me, I chose to play it safe. Perhaps it was because I was getting over a cold as to why I chose to be selective with my personal style of dress. I wasn't prepared to shed the winter clothing so soon, despite the fact that the sun was shining ever so brightly.

The sun had everyone drumming to a different beat, a more upbeat one that welcomed change. For everyone now took the time out of their busy schedule to actually acknowledge each other with either a quick hello or even a warm smile, as opposed to people passing one another in a nonresponsive manner or exchanging the sometimes reciprocated empty, cold stares that people so often gave. So what allows one to behave in such a manner?

Normally either people resist, like I did when I chose to play it safe and wear a coat despite the fact that the sun was shining, or people can go the other way, so to speak, and embrace and celebrate change, like so many of the other people who chose to wear shorts and brightly colored clothing. When this altercation or modification occurs in your life, like the changing of the winter months to the spring months, you may opt to look backward and below or spring forward and above.

Take, for instance, something as simple as paying attention to your steps when walking while the sun is out. What usually happens when you look down?

Well, normally a dark area or shape produced by your body appears, which is referred to as a shadow. That is created because our bodies have come between rays of light and the sidewalk surface. Similar to the shadows of doubt, fear, or unhappiness, all these things may come between the rays of light. However, if given a chance, the beam will shine even brighter in our lives than any shining star.

The same can be said with the test, trials, tribulations, or mountains that are present in our lives. We can choose to have these things physically, emotionally, spiritually beat us up, or we can choose to fight to keep the hope alive and ultimately have beams of light constantly shine down on us so that we are no longer seeing the shadow.

Rich Thoughts

When have you had to leave the past behind (your shadow) and move toward a higher height of optimism?

_____

_____

_____

_____

_____

_____

_____

_____

_____

_____

_____

Rich Point for Your Day

Today I will look toward my shadow; I will look toward the sunshine in the clouds.

Life is RICH when you are able to acknowledge that . . .

His favor surrounds us like a shield.

Every morning before my feet touch the floor, I say out loud, "Thank you, Father, for another blessed day." I thank him for making me righteous and that I have favor with everyone that comes into contact with me for that particular day. I pray that people will go out of their way not only to help me but also to listen to me and bless me abundantly and furthermore to allow the doors that were once closed to now miraculously be opened.

Although I do not have any enemies that I am aware of, I also thank him, for if it were not because of my Father's tender mercies, my enemies would have triumphed over me. I also continue to declare restoration to everything that has been stolen from me. I thank him that in the midst of my test, trials, and tribulations that I am still able to see my Heavenly Father's face. And because of this, I have great turnarounds and breakthroughs despite what has been sighted from one's naked eyes and because of this. HIS favor is truly awesome!

Today was no different than any other day, only that I had wanted to order a muffin and a cup of hot chocolate for my son for his breakfast during our stay at a hotel. I had only a certain amount of money and I began to think if the money would be enough to cover the food items and the delivery room service fee as well. I remember speaking to the gentlemen in the room service department. He had asked me if I had only wanted one muffin. My reply remained the same. However, when he came to our hotel suite, I sighted three muffins, and when I asked him how much was owed to him, he beckoned for me to look down at the bill. That is when I saw that it was half of the expected amount. I commenced to ask this blessed soul from the room service department why there were three muffins. His response was that they were small and wanted to give more. I gave him the expected change and told him how grateful we were and told him to have a blessed day.

What happened in the hotel room that morning reminded me of the importance of continuing to give thanks to God. It was also a reminder to me that I no longer have to fight, for he fights each and every one of my battles every day, all the time, every hour, every minute, and every second. And because he does this for me, I know that his favor surrounds me as a shield. This shield allows me to commence each journey with single steps of faith so that I may propel forward with the many journeys that are predestined for my life. Each day I am made more and more aware that there are angels placed here on earth that divinely intervene on my behalf. Unexplainable things happen that can only be explained by the works of his mighty hand. Strength and courage are infused into every pore into my body, which allows me to move forward when I deem myself as being spiritually and physically weak. That, my friends, is the works of our Jehovah Jirah.

It is vitally important to continue to give thanks even in the midst of your trials and tribulation. Begin each day with the thought that you are blessed and highly favored. Continue to give thanks without ceasing.

I still cry out to God and thank him once more for all that he has done for me and my family. This was truly a testimony to how his favor surrounds us with his shield. Let him do the same for you.

Rich Thoughts

When has the Creator shielded you with his favor?

_____

_____

_____

_____

_____

_____

_____

_____

_____

_____

_____

_____

Rich Point for Your Day

Today I will experience the free favors of God that profusely and lavishly abound on my behalf.

Life is RICH when you are able to acknowledge that . . .

Courage is being able to go where there is no path.

Gathering strength in the face of adversity is not as easy as many would like to believe, because it requires an individual to nerve oneself to do something that usually frightens them. This path of fear may lead us to unexpected obstacles, which may even provide roadblocks and, as a result, prevents you from arriving to your sought-out destination on time and with care. Holding on to that particular pain or issue that gives you grief is not always a sign of being strong. Sometimes it takes more strength and courage to just let go.

I too had to make that conscious decision to just let go of the things that were giving me grief. It was not easy but rather necessary for any new transformation to truly take place in my life.

I had been signed up to participate in a course that spoke to chronic pain management. Upon completion I would be certified to be a peer leader trainer, and the thought of having such an accolade attached to my person sounded absolutely ambitious on the one hand, and on the other, it sounded quite intimidating to be in the company of others. But now having looked back on how things panned out, I would have to say that it was an experience that brought forth such a magnitude of richness that helped me to *just let go*. I had been an educator for fourteen years who conducted workshops, gave lectures, planned and organized many school events, and coached, and I was a student teacher mentor / host teacher and principal designate for years, yet the thought of having to sit among strangers, read through and interpret their findings, and teach to a small group of participants frightened me a great deal.

I have always spoken about the angels placed here on earth who have either breathed life back into me or who have spoken some words of wisdom that allowed self-reflection. On my part, however, this one women's company in particular taught me many things. The one that stood out the most for me was the words she chose to use and refer to: "to surrender to it all."

Because of the driving anxieties that I had developed after the motor vehicle accident, this kind soul picked me up every session and drove me to the destination for this course, then back home again. Little did she know that each journey allowed me to gather greater strength so that I was finally able to seek out my expected destination on time and with care. We spoke about the art and power of communication and how much our lives had changed due to the fear of pain. She spoke about continuing to chase after dreams and never losing sight of them and taught me once more that it was okay to not always have the solution to everyone else's problem. We laughed, vented, and learned how important it is to just let go.

At the chronic pain management sessions, all participants had an amazing story to tell. I believe that it was the sharing of those stories that allowed this journey to be even richer than I had intended it to be. We came from different walks of life, yet we shared a commonality of courage. We took a different path that we had never taken before.

Our instructor was phenomenal and I saw many star qualities in her that *others* had seen in myself. She was patient and thorough in everything that she delivered to the group. It was only when she informed us that, for the upcoming session, we would have to teach that I felt ill and paralyzed with fear. It was only after having mustered up the courage and strength to just let go of these feelings or debilitating thoughts did I realize that this territory was not so unfamiliar after all. I taught well with ease like a pro.

I was forced to nerve myself into teaching that had such a frightening grip on me for so many years. However, by taking this new path, it allowed me to lead myself to the unexpected obstacles of facing my self-fears. I learned that I was my own roadblock, and as a result, I had learned that I was the one who had prevented myself all these years from arriving to my sought-out destination on time and with care.

Rich Thoughts

When have you had to be courageous? How did you accomplish this?

_____

_____

_____

_____

_____

_____

_____

_____

_____

_____

_____

_____

Rich Point for Your Day

Today I will be courageous and continue to take the trail that leads to the path of strength.

Life is RICH when you are able to acknowledge that . . .

Our eyes are the windows to the soul.

When I was a child and told a *little lie* and would later have had to confront an adult, I would rarely look them in their face. Although many would see this as a form of disrespect or perhaps even being an indication of being a tad shy, little did they know that the reason why I would look toward the ground was to save myself from possibly being found out and ultimately punished by one of them.

You see, for others it may be their body language or even their tone of voice that would give them away. But for me, they were my eyes. Therefore, when I was asked if I had known anything about the whereabouts of my new winter boots, how the cookies had finished so quickly when they had only been purchased the day before, or who drew on the wall with the Crayola crayons, my eyes made no contact with the *prosecutor* who was asking these questions. I would give a response that was half-true, and although I was taught to speak the truth, I chose to do otherwise and be on my merry way. Little did I know that the adults always played this game titled "play fool to catch wise." For when I thought that I was outsmarting them, they had already known the truth. I had always wanted to know how *they* had known. And as I got older and wiser, I knew that my eyes were most definitely the windows to my soul. And because of this, my eyes continued to be the ones that usually gave me away. Because they knew me so well, they were able to see right through me. I also found out that the reason why they were so ahead of me in the winning of this game titled "play fool to catch wise" was because they had once played the exact games too.

Rich Thoughts

Have you ever found it difficult to look someone in the eye when having to tell him or her something devastating? Why?

_____

_____

_____

_____

_____

_____

_____

_____

_____

_____

_____

Rich Point for Your Day

Today I will be conscious of my eyes and allow truth to represent my soul.

Life is RICH when you are able to acknowledge that . . .

Relaxation is the key for RICH results.

I have always been the kind of woman who has always appreciated having baths much more than taking showers. So locking myself away in my sanctuary, free from any disturbances or noise, sounded like a superb idea for me. The was my secret place—the bathroom, void of any conversations that included the following dialogue—"Mom, do you know where I can find some socks?" or "Babes, did you see my boxers?"—was like heaven for me. For as women, we can wear so many hats that, if you are not careful, the hats that you wear may consume your ability to find solace within yourself.

And as I look around *my* bathroom, I think that I have done pretty well in accomplishing that atmosphere that evokes peace and tranquility. For not only were there lit candles strategically placed alongside the bathtub, my bathwater consisted of Epsom salts and lots of lavender-scented bubbles. As my weary body became submerge into the depths of this much-needed form of relaxation, all the cares of the world were slowly washed off my entire body. In doing so, I would exhale.

Who would have ever known that water could feel so good! Having said that, my bathroom became and continues to be my haven because I find solace and usually receive the answers to my questions by merely sitting in silence in the water.

These tranquil moments allow me to become one in mind, body, and spirit. My breathing brings me to a place of restoration and connects my thoughts with peace. So I find myself making it more of a habit to treat myself to more of these bath escapades in hopes of being a better and more relaxed person.

Rich Thoughts

List some of the things that you do that allow you to relax.

_____

_____

_____

_____

_____

_____

_____

_____

_____

_____

_____

_____

_____

Rich Point for Your Day

Today I choose to participate in the activities that promote the relaxation of self.

Life is RICH when you are able to acknowledge that . . .

You must always entertain your inner child.

Watching my husband in a Toys "R" Us store is the most amusing sight to see, for he goes down every aisle looking at the contents, wide-eyed and bushy-tailed, as if he were five years old again. His excuse for this childish behavior and excitement is that he has to touch and play with all the gadgets, toys, and remote control cars so that our *son* will appreciate the craftsmanship of these toys. The truth of the matter is that he is the one who seems to be more interested in these items.

And now that our son is twelve years old and is entering the realm of the teenager world, he continues to get excited when seeing these toys. His rationalization for this is that our son would absolutely love them, but we both know that it is only because he, my husband, absolutely loves them. Therefore, the saying "Once a man, twice a child" suits him perfectly. For if we did not entertain our childlike appetite, I believe that we would be more miserable and more prone to having to accept the complexity of life in all its forms.

All in all he should be commended for being able to find enjoyment in these toys while he satisfies his boyish appetite. I believe that this is his secret in maintaining that *innocence* to life and all that it has to offer.

Rich Thoughts

How does the saying "Once a man, twice a child" relate to you?

_____
_____
_____
_____
_____
_____
_____
_____
_____
_____
_____
_____

Rich Point for Your Day

Today I will do all the things that I found pleasure in as a child so that I may continue to quench the thirst of my childhood.

Life is RICH when you are able to acknowledge that . . .

Warnings are to protect us, not to punish us.

We are surrounded by unseen danger that may ultimately endanger our lives and even our relationships; yet we fail to understand that these unseen dangers do not come from outside of us; they reside in us.

We had noticed a change in our son's behavior, yet we could not pinpoint the reasons as to why this change was coming about. We would ask him continuously if he had missed his grandparents who recently relocated to the Caribbean. Or maybe it was because of all the things that took place after the motor vehicle accident, which attributed to this distance we were observing. We asked our son if it was because of the losses of the babies after we shared the news of having heard the heartbeats. We even asked him if this newfound behavior had come about because we had sold our home and now had to live among family members and stay in the occasional hotel, or if it was the recent deaths of our so many loved ones. We asked and asked and asked him what was wrong. To them all, our son's response was nothing and that he was fine.

We spoke to a few friends and family members, all of whom verbalized the importance of keeping the ties of communication open with our child. Needless to say, these unseen dangers that were beginning to endanger our son's life and our relationship with one another became confusing and overwhelming. We began to seek out prayers for protection and for some sort of revelation as to what would possibly be the main culprit to our concerns.

Slowly things began to unravel and our son began to talk—not face-to-face but via text. What we thought was just a teenage phase was a little more serious than what we could ever imagine.

The unseen dangers from the outside (our son's behavior) acted as a warning to us in the sense that it alerted us that something was not right. It just so happened that our son was being bullied and kept his thoughts about what was happening to himself until that day when he had felt uncomfortable to tell us what was really going on. Our son was extremely angry, resentful, and frustrated. The bully was a so-called friend but always took things too far. Our son acted out in a manner that was foreign for him and also foreign for us. These warnings protected us but caused a lot of sleepless nights, anguish, and ceaseless prayer for our son.

These warnings allowed our son to be protected in a strange way, for we were able to discuss our concerns with both the principal and the vice principal and the boy who was bullying our son. Our son no longer was being punished, nor were we. In a strange way we were being protected from what could have been detrimental if the warning signs were ignored a little while longer. We sighted these dangers from the outside and quickly addressed the unforeseen dangers of anger that our son displayed in response to this circumstance. By being able to deal appropriately with the unforeseen danger that resided within him, we learned that a continuous open communication with our son is needed in order to ensure his protection.

Rich Thoughts

When have you chosen to ignore warning signs?

_____

_____

_____

_____

_____

_____

_____

_____

_____

_____

_____

_____

Rich Point for Your Day

Today I will not grumble at the warning signs, but will proceed with caution.

Life is RICH when you are able to acknowledge that . . .

A symphony of stars depicts how great God is.

Being a city dweller does not always allow you to appreciate Mother Nature for her truly splendid beauty. And because of this, I envy the people that reside up north, for they are always enveloped in the things that we would not normally see, hear, or feel.

The pace of life, the air we breathe, and the northern skies are all very different in comparison to our fast-paced city life, which is often riddled with smog and dimly lit polluted skies.

I fell in love with the sky and everything within it when I had had the opportunity to see Halley's Comet in the late nineties. It was the dead of winter and we had to wait a few hours in our snowsuits outside in the frigid temperatures with the others who shared a fascination for the skies and the stars. However, the waiting to experience such a wonderful sight was all worth our while. There is something about looking up into the sky that night and being able to see an entirely different world of newfound possibilities. It was quite mystical, if you ask me.

That was almost fifteen years ago, yet I still remember it quite vividly as if it were yesterday. Today I have the opportunity again, maybe not to sight the infamous Halley's Comet but to sight the various constellations in the sky from another part of the world. This year the entire family was spending Christmas break in the Caribbean at our parents' home in Montego Bay Jamaica. There is something that is rather appealing and breathtaking about where Mommy and Daddy's house is situated. A long winding private road with palm trees strategically placed along the way up, huge metal gates midpoint between the road and the house, and then some more palm trees met with a beautiful garden filled with exotic and colorful flowers right in front of the house—those sights during the day are sights to see, but the sight that one captures during the night is to die for.

This extended musical composition of the blacked sky, with the many stars scattered throughout the quiet skies, played a melodic musical piece for me each and every night. It reminded me of how great God is and how magnificent he always will be. For he created all these majestic and phenomenal things—the symphony of the stars—and because of this creation, HE is the composer of everything beneath the skies.

So although many may take for granted the ability to see what the skies have to offer, I will always find a deep-seated appreciation for not only the composer, but the symphony of stars.

Rich Thoughts

When is the last time that you have observed the stars in the sky?

_____

_____

_____

_____

_____

_____

_____

_____

_____

_____

_____

_____

Rich Point for Your Day

Today I will remember that the sky remains a symphony of excellence.

Life is RICH when you are able to acknowledge that . . .

We delight in the beauty of the butterfly.

Butterflies are absolutely beautiful. Well, to me they are. They hold a special place within my heart and will continue to exemplify so much more than beauty. For me butterflies represent change in the advent of adversity, and because of this, I chose to have one inked on my skin to remind me of the loss of my second child. Just like the butterfly, I too went through an enormous amount of change before I could accept the beauty of what life had to offer in the midst of so much grief and pain.

Rarely does one admit the changes it must go through in order to achieve this impressive exquisiteness, and because of this, I admire them even more for the butterfly represents me.

Just as how it started out as a caterpillar, then as a cocoon, then transforming into a butterfly, I too went through this change.

I had floated free of time, carrying hopes for many things in my life—love, joy, and celebration. Like this blessed creature, I too aspired to flutter and savor each moment as it passes. I was used to embracing all that life had to offer; however, celebrating the joy of everyday life became too hard for me to endure. This transformation and moment in my life reminded me that life is rich and that beauty is and was everywhere.

That year, I was reminded of how beautiful butterflies truly are. On a daily basis, whether it was early in the morning, in the afternoon, or in the earlier part of the evening, a monarch butterfly or any other butterfly would flutter in front of me. It could be when I was driving, walking, or just sitting outside. I do not take those occurrences lightly, for in my eyes, it spoke to my life and continues to speak to my current situation.

For every personal connection took on a rather different meaning, and the laughter of life's creation was delightfully the sweetest for me.

Just like the butterfly, I am moving through different life cycles, and not only have I tuned in to my emotional state but I have tapped into my spiritual state as well because finding joy in life and lightness are very important to me.

Rich Thoughts

Have you gone through any life transformations lately? Which stage best described that change?

_____

_____

_____

_____

_____

_____

_____

_____

_____

_____

_____

_____

Rich Point for Your Day

Today if I am to see a butterfly, I will remind myself of all the necessary changes I too must endure in order to be beautiful.

Life is RICH when you are able to acknowledge that . . .

Hope has power.

Every morning I made it a habit to take some time out from my busy schedule to say thank you to my Heavenly Father. I began familiarizing myself with this habit and would read a few scriptures from the Bible and listen to some gospel songs. What tugged most at my heartstrings were the scriptures that I read from the book of Romans 5: 1–4:

Therefore, having been justified by faith, we have peace with God through our Lord Jesus Christ, through whom also we have obtained our introduction by faith into this grace in which we stand; and we exult in hope of the glory of God. And not only this, but we also exult in our tribulations, knowing that tribulation brings about perseverance; and perseverance, proven character; and proven character, hope.

This passage spoke mountains to my situation. What a great reminder and what a great lesson for us all to remember the importance of walking by faith and not believing what we see that is normally presented to the naked eye. For when we are physically unable to see what lies before us, we become discouraged. However, when we have access to faith, the tribulations that we are faced with allows us to develop perseverance.

These feelings or expectations and desires for the certain things I yearned to manifest no longer became something that I wanted. To hope for all to be well slowly became loosened from my feeble grasp.

I became numb and therefore I lacked the power to hope and therefore lost my way to navigate through the daily liberties of life. I was tired of having to go through the many scheduled MRIs, x-rays, assessments, and appointments with the specialists and doctors.

I was tired of having to visit the different hospitals each week. I was tired of the scheduled discovery meetings and lawyer appointments and tired of having my hopes up, believing that the ending of all this crap would be near. My hopes for all the madness of someday coming to a complete halt continued to be merely a distant distraction from what I wanted the truth to really be.

Slowly but surely these feelings or expectations and desires to *life* became part of *my* equation again to just hold on. By being able to trudge through whatever is presented to you in faith, our character becomes redefined, and once our character has been cultivated, the hope to carry on in the midst of our obstacles becomes more attainable.

Rich Thoughts

Was there ever a time when all hope was gone?

_____
_____
_____
_____
_____
_____
_____
_____
_____
_____
_____
_____

Rich Point for Your Day

Today I am reminded that, if we hope for what we do not see, we eagerly wait for it with perseverance.

Life is RICH when you are able to acknowledge that . . .

You are to hold your loved ones close to your heart.

When I learned of my grandmother's death, my entire body became numb with a wealth of emotions. I felt paralyzed of having to entertain the thought that another loved one whom I hold dear to my heart will no longer be here.

I am now left with the multitude of memories of this great woman, who not only exemplified the epitome of strength but shared her wisdom and always allowed her beauty to shine brighter than any diamond. This woman that I speak of and refer to is my grandmother—Mrs. Gladys Smart.

I am so blessed to have been able to meet her, to know her, to love her, and to develop that bond that so many grandchildren yearn to have.

Although I could not physically see her on a daily basis, her presence was always with me. At times I would call out her name or think of her and literally see us during my childhood days, teenage, and adult years. I would see all the times that I spent during the summer months or the occasional March and Christmas breaks in Jamaica. These candid moments would flood my memory like the depths of the deepest ocean.

There is no doubt in my mind or within my heart, the love I have for my grandmother. Despite the fact that she could not hold a conversation with me the last time I saw her, I truly believe that she recognized me. We communicated in our own way. My grandmother spoke to me through the art of touch. For when I held her hand, she held on to mine and didn't let go.

Although it was a very difficult time for us to see her go, and although the tears that fell from our eyes and the pain that burst within our hearts remain to be laden with sadness and grief, I know that she is in a better place, free of pain, hurt, or disappointment. So I have decided that, on that day my grandmother was laid to rest, I would not say good-bye. For every time that I would see the sunrise or sunset, every time that I would see the stars illuminating in the sky, and every time I would think of a grandparent's love, I will always think of her.

My dearest grandmother, I would like to say thank you, thank you for the many life lessons you have taught me.

Rich Thoughts

Write about a fond memory that you have shared with your grandparent.

_____

_____

_____

_____

_____

_____

_____

_____

_____

_____

_____

_____

Rich Point for Your Day

Today I will absorb myself in the memories of my grandmother and find refuge, knowing that she will live forever within my heart.

Life is RICH when you are able to acknowledge that . . .

Quiet times of prayer connect us with God.

Many people have not learned how to appreciate having a bit of quiet time for we live in a fast-paced society, community, and world that caters to embracing the fact that being busy is a good thing. We tend to always celebrate having to be in the presence of others, and therefore it renders a sense of unfamiliarity and uneasiness.

However, as far as I can remember, I have always loved to maintain a balance of the two. I enjoyed the company of others, while other times I chose to savor the moments of being alone and learned to love every moment of those quiet time experiences. Having the opportunity to regularly connect with myself, whether it be sessions of spiritual activities, such as prayer or mindful meditation, I find that having those moments with self has allowed me to connect to my Creator. In doing so, it not only provided me with access and communication with HIM, but it allowed me to express how thankful I am for HIM and every situation I am immersed in, whether it was for the good or not for the betterment of my well-being.

It was the evening before my birthday, and I had mapped out how everything would be. My girls and I were going to go out to a pole dancing party for me, then come back to my home for some more fun and also for a late-night dinner. My husband and son had already decided that that night would be my night with the girls and would grant me the so well-deserved time with them to catch up and celebrate my day. It was fabulous, to say the least. We bonded, we laughed, we drank, we ate, and we had intense conversations about God.

It was getting late and my husband wanted to know how much longer I would need for my girls' date/birthday night, for he did not want to rein in on my parade. My response was for him and our son to come home, for they had not seen the girls in a long while. Needless to say, it was the best evening I had in a long time because I was able to spend it not only with my friends but with my loved ones. What took place thereafter truly was a testimony of all our connections with God.

Some of us sat on the sofa, while others sat on the floor among some of the pillows that were placed on the sofa. However, we were all in close proximity of each other. We all turned within to that quiet place and the quiet time began.

This happened simply intentionally having conversations with God. Those that felt the urge to speak did so, while others listened to HIS voice through the prayers that were spoken. The solemn request for help, strength, and protection and expressions of thanks were truly phenomenal. It electrified the room and immediately touched each individual present. This session of private mediation bought us all together in a way that left us feeling tremendously overwhelmed with emotions. God is so good to us, for he does hear our voices and sees our every tear that has been shed. HE knows our heart and most definitely hears our prayers.

Rich Thoughts

How often do you turn within?

_____

_____

_____

_____

_____

_____

_____

_____

_____

_____

_____

_____

_____

Rich Point for Your Day

Today I will make a conscious effort to connect more with the Creator through prayer.

Life is RICH when you are able to acknowledge that . . .

We are all queens.

The world enjoys capitalizing and cashing in on all these *special* days. The Hallmark stores become flooded with the many sentimental cards, plush toys, mugs, and all the other goodies that are normally sold in celebration of these days.

Not only do we have an appreciation day for teachers, we also honor our grandparents, our fathers, and of course, our beloved mothers. And although the mothers are important even after this *day* comes to an end, we should continue to capture these Hallmark moments each and every day, if not by others, then by ourselves.

I truly believe that women should be treated like queens every day, all day, because we do so much! Besides, that is the way I was treated when I was growing up. So to say the least, I expected it to remain this way. So I continue to get the carefully picked bouquet of roses or an orchid every once in a while, and if they are not bought for me that particular week, I buy them for myself. Nothing is wrong with this, because part of the queen code of conduct is to take care of yourself at all times spiritually, emotionally, and yes, physically as well. That is why from time to time, I either get treated or treat myself to a massage or a manicure or pedicure and schedule a visit to my naturopathic doctor, and perhaps that is one of the main reasons as to why I am ever so conscious of the foods that are placed into my temple. We are all queens, and the maintenance of such a prestigious title requires a lot of work in order to be most effective.

Finding that balance in your life, and being able to maintain it, is a must. Or else it becomes rather difficult for you to be your best. Do whatever it takes to love and appreciate yourself, whether by receiving or writing positive inspirational affirmations and speaking them into your life on a daily basis, or writing love letters to yourself if no one else is doing that for you, or filling the bathtub with rose petals surrounded with lit scented candles. Take charge of you and your palace, reclaim your throne, and reign like the queen that you are.

Rich Thoughts

What qualities of a queen do you have?

_____
_____
_____
_____
_____
_____
_____
_____
_____
_____
_____
_____

Rich Point for Your Day

Today I will remember that I am a descendant of royalty.

Life is RICH when you are able to acknowledge that . . .

Your steps of uniqueness lead you to your journey of creativity.

Whether or not you are aware of your steps, each one that you take and make defines your uniqueness! Your steps may consist of a walk, a jog, or even a run. However, you must remember that each one of those steps requires you to visit that foreign territory.

Visual arts classes were fun and exciting. I always looked forward in attending these sessions in hopes of learning something even more unique and outside of the box than the previous class that I had attended the week before. The students would dabble in all areas associated with the elements and principles of design and would showcase our talent by incorporating what we had learned from our instructor into our art compositions.

Long after I had stopped taking the visual arts classes, the metacognitive skill and art of visualization remained to be part of me. When I would read a novel or hear the lyrics to a song, I would visualize everything from the plot, the setting, and the characters. I prefer reading a novel and would chose one any day over watching the movie written from the book. For I enjoyed seeing the world come to life through my eyes!

As an educator, the visualization trait assisted me in creating and writing fun learning lesson plans and activities for students. I could see things, and because of this gift, I turned the visions I had of certain things in my mind into a reality. Little did I know that these steps of uniqueness from my childhood, teenage years, adult life as an educator, and even my motor vehicle accident, were setting me up for a journey of creativity. The gift to see . . .

My motor vehicle accident was a life-changing event that happened to me. It transformed me in every area of my life. However, those dark experiences birthed a great opportunity for me to share my story and equip others to heal as they make their way through their journey. I had a vision to help other women who had gone through similar traumatic events as I had. I had a vision to create programs and a safe/loving environment for women to know that they are not alone. I had a vision, and I believed, and I succeeded when I was able to see my unique experiences of trauma, depression, love, pain, fear, and faith leading me on the path of creativity that enabled me to heal.

Rich Thoughts

What makes you unique?

_____

_____

_____

_____

_____

_____

_____

_____

_____

_____

_____

_____

Rich Point for Your Day

Today I will allow my steps to lead me to a place of creativity where I have never gone before.

Life is RICH when you are able to acknowledge that . . .

Your beam of light will never grow dim only if you let it.

We were awakened by the footsteps of our twelve-year-old son approaching our bedroom, reminding us of the time and that we could not be late for the seven o'clock morning bus pickup at his school.

Today was the day that the grade 8 students from his school would venture up north for three days and two nights to participate in leadership skills and team building activities that would mold them into teenagers who would think more effectively and implement the learning of these seven habits into their lives more with ease.

Although quite groggy and wanting to have the option to roll over and taking in a few more *zzzzzs*, it continued to be that of a mere fantasy rather than a reality for me, it often seems.

He was excited underneath all that machismo that I am relearning that all teenagers commence to adapt at this, shall I say, less-than-joyous growing-up phase.

All in all, I was elated to know that he was feeling this way and knew that this day was off to a wonderful start. I know this because, when I looked out the window of our dining room area, the sight that I saw was absolutely breathtaking and reminded me of a very important message.

We followed through with our daily routine, and then we were out the door. We accomplished our mission and our son arrived on time at school. I on the other hand could not shake the beautiful scenery I sighted that morning and more importantly the inspirational message that spoke to me.

For the past few months I battled with depression and posttraumatic stress, and because of this, my vision became cloudy and my light, so to speak, had been turned down low. The things that I enjoyed doing and the people with whom I enjoyed sharing my time with no longer became exciting or important to me. For I found solace in being by myself and enjoyed the darkness. I no longer beamed for the things in life that gave me great joy and happiness. My actions, thoughts, and behaviors now grew dimmer and brought me to a place of deep despair. It was only having a conversation with a family friend did I learn the importance of staying in the light when faced or surrounded by darkness. "Turn on that light," she said into the receiver. "And remain standing in it." So I did just that. So when I saw the ray of sunlight bursting through the clouds as the day continued to get brighter with each passing moment. I was able to make a connection to myself that the clouds of darkness and despair where slowly dissipating because of that one beam of light that never gave up. In doing so, I saw that breakthrough and understood that my beam of light will never grow dim only if I let it, and therefore I choose for it not to, not anymore.

Rich Thoughts

Has your light ever been turned down low, and if so, what did you do have to do in order for it to be turned up again?

_____

_____

_____

_____

_____

_____

_____

_____

_____

_____

_____

Rich Point for Your Day

Today I will remain in the light, even when things get dim.

Life is RICH when you are able to acknowledge that . . .

You outnumber the stars in the sky.

One night we decided to take a drive down to one of our recent spots that overlooked the lake. I remembered us locating a spot and sitting on one of the huge rock deposits that Mother Nature had purposely laid for this very purpose. As we sat and talked outside in the crisp yet refreshing midnight air. It remained unfathomable to me how beautifully lit the skies could get, for it was as if our Creator went into a jar full of stars and scattered them throughout the galaxy. There seemed to be more than one hundred million of these sparkling objects everywhere, every night that we choose to visit these hidden gems, and to say the least, I was starstruck and stood in awe of their incandescent presence every visit.

We continued our family rendezvous among the stars in the sky and talked about everything under the moon related to our dreams and the importance of continuing to shine brighter than any star.

That night we spent a couple of hours underneath an umbrella of magnificent stars. In doing so, it reintroduced the possibility of hope and faith to the things that once lost their luster for life. I am thankful for that particular moment because, in my adversity, I learned to be thankful even when things had looked grim. Looking up into the sky and then seeing the stars brought things into greater perspective for me and reminded me that this florescent light was a path that became symbolic to my own vision and reminded me to never give up on my dreams, because I was beginning to understand that one's dreams may not always be embraced and celebrated as you might have hoped for. But that night, I was encouraged to see the galaxy, in this case the bigger picture, interpret and ponder about everything that I kept dear to my heart, and then synthesize it all in relation to me.

The stars in the sky allowed me to think about my thinking and everything that was and became entangled within my frame of thought. In doing so, these endless thoughts allowed me to continue searching for that light that shone so bright in the darkest moments in my life. The constellations of stars reminded me that I am wonderfully made and have a lot to offer the world, despite what others may feel.

Although the visibility of the stars in the sky are clearly seen by the naked eye in the country side, as opposed to the city, that did not mean that they were not there. And this is exactly what my point is for you. We should always remember that each and every one of us has a special gift and hold special talents that are waiting to be tapped into. However, at times I believe that we tend to sometimes *overlook* these special gifts and talents when we relate it back to ourselves. Let today be the first of the last, where you begin to allow the clamor of someone else's opinion and insecurities to dim your light. Instill within yourselves the importance of creating some goals about how you are going to reconstruct your thinking of how you will outnumber the stars in the sky.

Rich Thoughts

Have you ever felt like your best was never good enough? What did you do to change this crippling thought?

_____

_____

_____

_____

_____

_____

_____

_____

_____

_____

_____

_____

_____

Rich Point for Your Day

Today I will remember that I OUTNUMBER the stars in the sky.

Life is RICH when you are able to acknowledge that . . .

Settling for second best is merely not good enough.

Being competitive in any area of our lives can be a good thing for achieving success while moving into the areas of glory and glamour. Not only can a competitive attitude help you feel energized but it allows you to take on challenging tasks that ultimately allow you to achieve the many things in life.

As long as I can remember, I have always been the competitive type. As a child I wanted to be better than the rest, whether in school, in extracurricular activities, or in the classroom, as I focused on the various aspects of my academic studies. I was competitive not only with others but with myself!

I loved to sleep, breathe, and eat everything associated with the recipe for achieving success. And this competitive attitude continued on throughout my teenage and into my adult life and as an educator.

I believe that taking on these challenging tasks in life allowed me to be the exemplary educator that I became. I wanted my students to excel. I wanted them to feel fun and thrive in a safe environment that would be conducive to higher learning. I wanted them to be challenged rhetorically and instilled the importance of having them constantly think about their thinking. In doing so, my motto for my students became these powerful words yet gentle reminders to the recipe of how to be successful—practice makes purpose. They should be leaders and not followers, and more importantly they should remember that their attitudes will always determine their altitudes.

That, my friends, can be remembered and applied to any person's life at any age—to not settle for second best.

So I continued to push myself by constantly reflecting on my teaching practices, taking new courses that spoke to differentiated learning and the various techniques educators may use in order to reach them. It was important to me that my students understood that hard work pays off and that, when I teach them, I see the face of my son. For as educators we have so much power and we have to be held accountable to our students because of the frightening factor that they can either make or break them. So I continue to learn twice, first as I prepare for my students, then as I teach them, because for me at least, settling for second best is merely not good enough.

Rich Thoughts

Have you ever settled for second best? If so, explain why using a few sentences.

_____

_____

_____

_____

_____

_____

_____

_____

_____

_____

_____

Rich Point for Your Day

Today I will not settle for anything else but the best.

Life is RICH when you are able to acknowledge that . . .

People are always watching.

Microscopes can be used for many things, but the sole purpose for one is to observe a given specimen. Just as how microscopes observe their specimen's every move, people do the same thing too. And the reality is, whether we like it or not, we will always be under a microscope.

Having said that, the importance of living a life full of respect, obedience, and kindness is perfectly suited. However, what happens when you don't live by the guidelines of the life previously mentioned but instead operate in a disrespectful, disobedient, and rather ill-mannered way? How will one be looked upon? How will one be judged? I believe that in both cases the person will be judged regardless of what has been presented. The viewers will see what they want to see. However, what we should keep in mind is that normally, when a specimen becomes magnified, you are able to observe things that could not be seen with just the naked eye. The same goes for people. We are too quick to judge a book by its cover and do not genuinely take into consideration the contents of the book. We do not appreciate or give credit to the fine details that have been put forth. Therefore, it is the responsibility of both the observed and the specimen under the microscope to be fair with what is being observed and what we are allowing others to see. For people are always watching.

Rich Thoughts

When you learn that someone is watching you, how do you react?

_____

_____

_____

_____

_____

_____

_____

_____

_____

_____

_____

_____

_____

Rich Point for Your Day

Today I will not get annoyed and will feel flattered to know that someone else feels it to be necessary for him or her to watch me.

Life is RICH when you are able to acknowledge that . . .

Worrying is a waste of time and energy.

People who worry for everything or who cannot find peace within themselves are pretty much like an infectious disease. Not only do they deplete themselves, they ultimately debilitate the people within their reach. Before even knowing what will transpire, they have already determined what the final outcome will be. These worry warts do not realize that, when they worry, it does not take away tomorrow's troubles; in fact it only persists to take away today's peace.

Although it may be difficult to do, I muster up everything in my power to not focus on worrying, because the final outcome of this is that it has affected my well-being not just physically but spiritually, mentally, and emotionally.

I find solace in the saying "With age comes maturity" because I would like to believe that the way that I deal with pressing issues then has taken a 360-degree turn from how I deal with the mountains that present themselves in my daily life today. I attribute this to finding the good in everything that presents itself to me. It sounds rather optimistic; however, with practice it brings forth purpose, and that purpose is to change or undo the habits that contributed to the worrying episodes. Even if it calls for me to worry, I breathe, think of whatever is ailing me, then try to let it go and try to learn what the lesson could possibly be for me. And when I look at this infectious disease in this manner, it no longer has its hold on me, and that is when I am able to understand on all levels how important it is not to worry, because it's just a waste of my precious time.

Rich Thoughts

When have you worried about something or fussed over someone?

_____

_____

_____

_____

_____

_____

_____

_____

_____

_____

_____

_____

Rich Point for Your Day

Today I will remember that, when I worry, it comes from a place of fear.

Life is RICH when you are able to acknowledge that . . .

Filling the void with stuff only complicates thing.

Complication arises when things are substituted with the Band-Aid approach. Lately things seemed to be going all wrong! And because of these changes, everything seemed to be an issue. Whether it was my inability to tolerate any form of foolishness or my inability to remain calm in any given situation, it was an issue, and if it was not this, then there was an argument about the most miniscule thing. At that time it remained to be a mystery as to why the important people in my life that I care so much about and love so deeply seemed to get so sensitive about everything underneath the moon and, on top of that, to behave so immaturely when we have to resolve matters.

It was only after that I was diagnosed with posttraumatic stress did the missing piece of the puzzle begin to make sense as to why things were the way they were.

I disliked everything that revolved around the motor vehicle accident because it left me with these changes that complicated things more than it needed to be. This traumatic event left me feeling frightened, sad, anxious, and at times disconnected to my surroundings and especially to my loved ones. I could not comprehend where these feelings of being alone came from and wanting to be alone despite being embraced with love.

Everything associated to this wretched day seemed to not fade fast enough for me, and the painful memories displayed in my mind and the pain that was felt within my body became a *part* of the new me.

Therefore, at that time the best learned mechanism for me to do in regards to this *stuff* was to go deep within—really deep within myself. I did not realize that, by doing this, I was only making things much worse not only for myself but painfully hard for my loved ones. But at that time I had the attitude of "Oh well, who cares" because it allowed me to cope with my stuff, and it felt good.

I now know that these feelings of intense distress when reminded of the trauma, the recent loss of interest in the activities that I once participated in, and the different outlook in life I now had were all attributed to being in a state of psychological shock as a result of my motor vehicle accident. Feeling detached from others, at times experiencing emotional numbness, becoming irritable, and having outbursts of anger that felt like they came from nowhere finally made sense to me.

Because I thought that seeking help was a sign of weakness, I did not get the help that I needed right away. It was only after becoming more educated to the symptoms and causes of posttraumatic stress did I become more comfortable with even speaking about it with some of my loved ones who did not even know. It is so natural to want to avoid painful memories or to even want to numb yourself for that matter; however, I learned that you cannot escape your emotions and that you can only push these feelings away for so long. And not only that, it becomes extremely exhausting, and many a times you end up harming your relationships, your ability to function, and your quality of life, which in the end is not worth it. So please seek the guidance and support that can mend you back to becoming whole, because filling the void with stuff only complicates things.

Rich Thoughts

Have you ever done something out of character to make up for the way you were feeling?

_____

_____

_____

_____

_____

_____

_____

_____

_____

_____

_____

_____

Rich Point for Your Day

Today I will not look toward something else to make up for a particular void in my life.

Life is RICH when you are able to acknowledge that . . .

Listening requires you to hear.

I find myself saying the exact same thing that my parents used to say to my siblings and to me: "If you can't hear, you will feel."

At first I didn't understand what they had meant until I was formally introduced to this phrase. Time and time again, I was reminded about the importance of hearing. I heard about it when I was a child and as a youth and have continued to hear about this as an adult. All in all, the connotation attached to this phrase has remained the same.

Listening is one of the most important skills you can have. How well you listen can literally affect every area of your life. Whether it be a requirement for your place of employment or with loved ones, we all must listen for this will have a profound effect on the relationships you have with others. However, there is a difference in being able to listen to what an individual has said and what an individual has actually heard.

As parents we not only have always taught our son to have a voice but emphasized the importance for him to listen, that he has two ears and one mouth. Hence we continue to explain to him the importance of him listening, and it may be beneficial for him to do so. For when you have heard, you have understood and applied it to whatever is required of you at that given point in time. However, when one listens, it literally goes in one ear and out the next.

What I have fallen victim to is that, because I am a parent and the adult, I have expected others, particularly our son, to listen to *me*. Where I find that this had become a problem is that I was listening to my son to obtain information and also for enjoyment but found that I failed terribly in the area of listening to him for *understanding*. Sad to say, I was not a very good listener and required a lot of help with the steps in practicing to become a better active listener. And because of the fact that subconsciously I did not hear the words that he was saying, I could not understand his complete message he was trying to convey.

I found it difficult to hear him because of all the distractions that were going on in and around me, and because of that, I felt that our son, who was taught to have a voice, became silenced, and the saying "If you can't hear, you will feel" became quite fitting to our mother-son relationship. So I began to "listen" to our son's body language again and noted my body language as well and made sure it was open and inviting to him, and began to reflect upon what our son had been saying and asked for clarity to certain points when I was unsure. It has been a challenge to undo an old habit, but I have made a conscious effort to listen more to him so that I could hear.

Rich Thoughts

Was there ever a time when it required you to really listen? Write a few sentences about that time.

_____

_____

_____

_____

_____

_____

_____

_____

_____

_____

_____

_____

Rich Point for Your Day

Today I will listen and then apply what I have heard to what is actually being said.

Life is RICH when you are able to acknowledge that . . .

The best is yet to come.

In the beginning stages of our dating relationship, the man who is now my husband had a plaque nailed to his bedroom wall that read, "Come walk with me, the best is yet to come." Although I understood what I read, I asked him what it meant. His response was that we should continue to walk with each other and be by each other's side and see what the future holds for the both of us. I have continued to walk with him, and I have also taken a few alternative routes on this journey. However, I frankly would not have it any other way. For strolling down the pathway and continuing on our journey of love with one another will always be forever.

Many people, or couples for that matter, do not have what we have. We have a rare kind of love that has been ignited by a flame that continued to grow brighter and brighter. Our walks have been encompassed with many seasons—seasons of stagnation and seasons of renewal and growth. However, throughout these seasons, we continued to work through them all by acknowledging them for what they truly signify. These walks were blessings in disguise that have taught us to be comforters to each other. In doing so, we have become each other's rock in times of need and continue to become closer and united each day in our choices of words that are spoken and in our actions and thoughts toward one another, which have allowed us to be fully equipped to take those walks into our future.

Rich Thoughts

Have you ever waited for the best to come and ended up with the worst?

Rich Point for Your Day

Today I will remind myself that sometimes the best does not come in a day or week. Sometimes the best comes in a month or a year, so hang tight.

Life is RICH when you are able to acknowledge that . . .

The impossible has made all things possible.

Motivational speakers encourage others to believe to succeed or believe to achieve the things that one would think to be out of one's reach. Interestingly enough, there seems to be many followers who also would like to see their dreams become a reality or to have someone encourage them to persevere and not lose sight of their unforeseen destiny.

Les Brown is one of those motivational speakers who continue to share his story, and he encourages others to find a means to their end. His messages are very powerful and allowed a dormant part of my being to be stirred with excitement.

I watched, listened, and heard the powerful messages his video "It's POSSIBLE" had sent to his viewers. It's amazing how much you forget that you are able to achieve your dreams if only you continue to persevere. Having that one person in your corner that believes in you as much as you do with your dream is a great asset. For I think that we tend to forget how powerful our minds really are and how true it is that failure is merely success turned inside out.

As I replayed this video another time, tears began to trickle down onto my face because, although I knew better, I too had thought that overcoming these never-ending tests, trials, and tribulations would never cease and that the once *impossible* would never become *possible* ever again.

These tears disproved my warped thoughts and allowed me to realize that I was alive and would continue to make my dreams a reality. It was only then did I realize that I had fallen so many times. Furthermore, I also realized that I had doubted so many times and I had sabotaged things so many times, but in the end I chose to stand and believe that in the word *impossible* reads the phrase "I'm possible!" From that time of rediscovery in the power to believe, I relearned that it was during those most difficult times of impossibility that a whole new/fresh world of possibilities became my reality, and because of that self-realization, I am most thankful for this day.

Rich Thoughts

Think about a time when the impossible was possible. Now write a few lines about how that felt.

_____

_____

_____

_____

_____

_____

_____

_____

_____

_____

_____

_____

Rich Point for Your Day

Today I will remain optimistic and remember that the impossible is very possible!

Life is RICH when you are able to acknowledge that . . .

Someone else's dreams are NOT your reality.

Parents always want the best for the children—the best life that they can possible give them, the best home that they can provide for them, and the best education that will lead to an outstanding profession.

I too fall within this category of wanting the best for my child. However, although we may want the best for our children, we still need to pay particular attention to these little peoples wants and needs.

When my son was around five years old, he had to prepare a speech for his teachers pertaining to what he wanted to become when he grew up. He chose to speak about wanting to become a doctor so that he could help the children who were suffering around the world, and at one point he wanted us to adopt a child because in his eyes it was simply unjust for anyone so young to suffer. He memorized his speech and did quite well, and as parents, we nurtured his aspirations despite having been only five years old. We bought doctor bags that contained all the doctor stuff one would use on their patients. We went to special exhibits that embraced his love for wanting to help others, and his personal doctors took the extra time to explain the diagrams on display that he was so intrigued with. They answered his never-ending questions that he always seemed to have about the functioning capability of some organ.

My son's love of wanting to help others continued, but now, instead of focusing on children, he wanted to help the homeless. If we were walking downtown and he would see a homeless person sitting on the sidewalk, he would ask for some money from us to give this person. We simply could not *ignore* his reality and the reality of this world.

Now being that he is in the intermediate grade, he has been encouraged to reflect upon his academic interests and future professional preferences. When asked if he still wants to become a doctor, his response to that question was that he wanted to become a software engineer. Although the visions of what he had wanted to become and what we had wanted him to pursue had changed, we welcomed the planting of his dream.

As parents although we want the best for our children, sometimes the best is not their best. We also understand that, like any other adult, he is allowed to change his mind and is allowed to chase after his dreams. More importantly we have understood that our dreams are not his reality, and because we want the best for our child, we therefore will continue to support our son in any way that we can so that his dreams embrace the notion of believing to achieve and succeeding as a software engineer.

Rich Thoughts

What are some of the things that you dream about?

_____

_____

_____

_____

_____

_____

_____

_____

_____

_____

_____

_____

Rich Point for Your Day

Today I will aim higher, shoot farther beyond the stars, and then believe to succeed.

Life is RICH when you are able to acknowledge that . . .

Angels are all around us.

Angels are often depicted as beings with bird-like wings on their back, halos, robes, and various forms of glowing light. However, what many people fail to realize is that angels protect and guide us in our daily lives and perhaps even carry out God's tasks, depending on your outlook to this topic of discussion.

Minibuses are not the main mode of transportation in the West Indies, but many people have relied on them throughout the years in order to take them to and from their chosen destination.

I personally dislike having to travel on them mainly because it does not matter how packed the buses may appear to be—there always seems to be room for just a few more. Just visualize a pack of sardines in a neatly packed tin. That is how I always feel when I have no other choice but to I travel on them. And although I love everything about the West Indies, I do not, however, like these minibuses that often are coupled with the occasional twists and turns that always drives at the speed of 140-ish kilometers per hour. That in itself is a recipe for disaster, meaning we arrived at the bus park a tad late.

The particular bus that we were to board on ironically had no more room for my husband, my son, and myself. So despite our disappointment of having to wait for a next bus, it seemed as if it worked out for the betterment of all of us. I believe we must have waited twenty additional minutes, which meant that our journey back into town would be a much longer treacherous ride. At one point, I just wanted to exit this contraption of speed and was satisfied to even walk. Realistically that would have taken me days to arrive at my desired destination. So to say the least, I held on tightly to whatever allowed me to. I pushed away the nauseated feelings and prayed that we would arrive safely. It was as if what I prayed for became our shield and protector in many ways than one. The driver of the minibus finally came to a complete halt, and that meant that I had some time to recuperate from the fast driving. However, when he remained at the same spot more than the expected time, everyone present on the bus began to question the extended stay. To our dismay, we learned that there was an accident a few meters from where we had been stationed. People in the community gathered together to give the other driver their assistance in moving their vehicle out from the road as it was blocking traffic in both directions. What my husband, son, and I learned is that the minibus that we were hurrying to board on (but were unable to because of the lack of room) was the vehicle that had gotten into a serious accident, which left some of the passengers jolted.

What took place was an act of God. We were most definitely protected by guardian angels and guided to safety. Our delay was our protection to what we witnessed that afternoon. There is no other explanation; angels are all around.

Rich Thoughts

Who do you think your guardian angels are?

_____

_____

_____

_____

_____

_____

_____

_____

_____

_____

_____

_____

Rich Point for Your Day

Today when I cannot make sense of the things that have happened, I will remember that there are angels all around me.

Life is RICH when you are able to acknowledge that . . .

You can run but cannot hide.

When you are running a race, there are many other participants, and depending on how you run, you will obtain something in exchange for your capabilities as a runner. Everyone competes for the prize. However, the runner who runs with uncertainty and fights for that prize and disciplines his or her body is the one who is the real champion, which leaves the other participants disqualified for the prize.

I have always enjoyed running. I participated in track and field in elementary and high school. However, when I entered university, I decided that I could not commit to the time and dedication the track coaches had wanted from me, for I did not think that I would be able to keep up with my studies while continuing on with such a rigorous training schedule. So I ran in a different light. I coached track and field for the students who attended the school when I became employed as a teacher. It was always rather interesting to meet the various participants at the first track and field tryouts. Having to judge one's performance is always a difficult thing to do. For one never truly knows one's "real" capability as a runner. Many coaches tend to be biased and use the previous years and equate how many first-place medals they had received.

My coaching or scouting tactics on the other hand were a little different from my colleagues' approach, in which I would not only look for that uncertainty but would search for the participants who were hungry and who were disciplined. These qualities to me were the real champions, the real winners, the ones who should be commended for their efforts. As time progressed, I learned to trust my instincts and the choices that I made in the decision process in regards to who would be chosen to be part of the team. I selected the participants who were often overlooked and not chosen right away because these participants were naturally the ones who turned out to be the real champions. When they would show up on time for practice, ready to train, these participants were the ones who took notes mentally and applied them to themselves. These were the participants who improved in each practice and continued to get faster and faster.

These are the ones who wanted to run away but in the end learned that they could not hide from the truth that disqualified the other participants for the prize. These participants persevered and became the real champions.

Rich Thoughts

When things get a bit unbearable, we tend to want to run away. Have you ever run away? If so, how far did you reach?

_____

_____

_____

_____

_____

_____

_____

_____

_____

_____

_____

_____

Rich Point for Your Day

Today I will remember that no matter how far I run, I will always be found.

Life is RICH when you are able to acknowledge that . . .

Laughter is the best remedy to life's ailments.

I didn't know that pictures could make someone laugh as hard as I heard my husband laughing. For some strange reason, I felt that the reason for these uncontrollable fits of laughter was because of one of my photos he sighted. I learned he was laughing at me that day, but I allowed it to happen just this one time because, when I sighted the photo and the shape of my face, I understood why he laughed; my side profile actually did resemble the shape of a banana! This did not offend me one bit though because we love to laugh. However, as of late, the laughter was not as half as consistent as it were around this time last year. So many losses, more specifically deaths, of close friends and loved ones really began to take their toll on the both of us.

My husband lost his only brother, his best friend, and I lost a brother-in-law and a teacher who rekindled the idea that it is simply okay to just laugh and to do so as if you have absolutely lost your entire mind. It pains me to know that Derrick is no longer here with us in the physical realm. We have definitely been left with a void that sometimes seems like it will never be filled, yet at the same time, with an overabundance of vivid memories of this gentleman's face and extreme kindness, we will continue to remember his laugh and remember his remarkable sense of humor. And more importantly we will forever cherish his undying love for his family.

It will never be an easy task to actually pick up the pieces of the once-complete puzzle of our lives and furthermore live the way we wished to do. However, as the days, weeks, months, and years went by, the ability to slide in a little chuckle here and a little smile there has paved a path to restoration. And in the midst of this realization comes forth acceptance—a newfound acceptance that Derrick would not want us to be sad or conduct ourselves in a manner that would compromise our joy or happiness within our lives.

Having said that, we sought out opportunity to correct our less-than-joyous habits that for too long silenced our laughter and ability to feel good. Hearing my husband's laughter and mine echoing his was the sweetest melody a song could make. It really was music to my ears and remains to be the best remedy to life's ailments.

Rich Thoughts

List a few of the things that make you laugh.

_____

_____

_____

_____

_____

_____

_____

_____

_____

_____

_____

_____

Rich Point for Your Day

Today I will laugh like no one is watching.

Life is RICH when you are able to acknowledge that . . .

Not being perfect is absolutely perfect.

In accordance with the website Freedictionary.com, the word *perfectionist* can be best delineated as "a person who is displeased by anything that does not meet very high standards." That definition pretty much sums up the person that I grew up to be. For as long as I can remember, I have always been that way, wanting to do well and doing everything in my power to excel far and beyond any given expectation. And because I became so displeased with anything that was not perfect, I became the one who could always do it right, on time and with care. I did it so well. My parents would say, "As long as you try and do the best that you can do"; that is all they every asked of me. So those words stayed with me, and I did just that—the best that I could do. I was always placed on a pedestal not only by my family members and loved ones but from my colleagues and friends.

I was the perfect wife, the perfect mother and daughter, the perfect granddaughter, sister, friend, colleague, and educator. Whether I was taking notes, studying, completing assessments, doing a job, practicing my piano lessons, and creating breakfast, lunches, or dinners, it had to be flawless, or else it just wasn't good enough, and back to the drawing board I would go.

Many people would assume being this way not to be healthy, but it worked for me, because that's all I have ever really known. It was only after my motor vehicle accident did I realize that I was no longer able to keep up with meeting these high standards. Because of the fact that that is all I've ever really known, when I couldn't, I became frustrated and felt like a failure, when in reality I was not.

Not being able to do the things that I was used to was very difficult for me. It was only after I had a conversation with my sister-in-law did I realize that not being perfect is absolutely perfect. She talked about whatever that could not be done on a particular given day was by no means a sign of being a failure. It simply meant, she went on to explain, that there is always a next day for completion of any task. So I have run with those words of wisdom and now bask in the delight knowing that not being perfect is absolutely perfect.

Rich Thoughts

Is there anything in this world that you consider to be perfect?

_____

_____

_____

_____

_____

_____

_____

_____

_____

_____

_____

_____

_____

_____

Rich Point for Your Day

Today I will remind myself that it is okay to not be perfect sometimes.

Life is RICH when you are able to acknowledge that . . .

Clearing the clutter is an absolute MUST.

Before feng shui became popular, there was me. I absolutely despise clutter for it truly alters my ability to focus on any task at hand. I could be at work, at home, or even at a restaurant for that matter, and if there were any form of clutter, I automatically would want to declutter.

Throughout my life, I have accumulated a lot of stuff. I have bins of things that have been collected throughout the years that I have deemed important to me, and because of its importance, each year it became that more difficult to get rid of those certain items. I really began to see how much clutter I accumulated after my parents gave me some of the bins they had stored at their home. They said that they were mainly articles and reading kits that I had kept from the various courses I had taken while I was in university. After seeing the bins, I had wished for them not to be in my possession. Where would I place these items now? Space for me was always an issue. I disliked confusion and this disordered state. Furthermore, the collection of these things did not help my situation at all; they just created a confused noise of clatter. So what I was forced to do next, I had no other choice but to do it. I created a master plan that all sounded good on paper, but the reality of it all was that it was much harder to do and required a lot of time to not only sort and sift but ultimately part with these things. What I thought would take a couple of hours actually took a few days, which stretched out as long as a month.

In the end I was able to recycle many things, give away some items, and housed the rest as keepsakes. I was able to get rid of the clutter that I had known of for so many years, although I no longer have certain items in my possession physically. I was able to hold on to those items via memories that I attached to each one of those stored items. It felt liberating to know that I was set free from holding on to the clutter. It also felt good to declutter too!

Rich Thoughts

Think of a time in your life when you had to declutter. How did you achieve this task?

_____

_____

_____

_____

_____

_____

_____

_____

_____

_____

_____

Rich Point for Your Day

Today I will work hard to declutter the cluttered areas of my life.

Life is RICH when you are able to acknowledge that . . .

Forced leisure is a significant pause that recaptures the necessities of one's life.

I don't think I have ever been the type of person who was able to fully relax. Not because I was a nervous person but because I always had a million and one things to do and prioritize my affairs well. Whether it was for the preparing of the usual things and routines that a wife and mother normally would do, preparing lesson plans, attending meetings, coaching, or delivering workshops as an educator, relaxing was definitely not in my vocabulary and it was a difficult thing for me to do. It got to the point where even sleeping in became something that I was unable to do.

I would do the odd thing for myself, whether it was having candlelit bubble baths, getting a manicure or pedicure, or simply venturing out to a bookstore and submerging myself among books. I would indulge in a little ME time from time to time but not as often as I would have liked to. I would often book an appointment to get some Reiki or massage done for me, yet this often resulted in me canceling the appointments due to being too busy. It was only when I was waiting for my son at his naturopathic and registered massage therapist appointment did I realize that I too deserve to take a break for myself, and I forced myself to recapture the experience of how it is to relax again because that existed in the far past and that past had been lost.

I decided to finally book an appointment for me with *them,* and everything about my appointment was perfect! Upon entering the office, the smell of a mixture of sage and lavender essential oils automatically welcomed and soothed my soul. The lighting, the setup, the questions, and my answers all pointed toward a time or opportunity of ease, relaxation, and freedom that was free from work or duties.

Learning how to slow down had to have been the most challenging thing that I have had to face, for I was always used to being on the go. However, now having the opportunity to have self-reflection, these quiet and rested moments allowed me to come to the knowing that there was a bigger plan for me. While getting my massage, I realized that for many years I had been walking around with a lot of pain, but I became so immune to it that I no longer recognized it. This visit was well needed, for with each touch and with each discussion, my body became more relaxed and hence more balanced with every passing minute.

I was quieted during those times; I had no other choice but to be. And during those moments of solitude, I began a journey that changed my life, I believe, for the better.

Now that I am back into my busy routine, I often pause to recapture the lessons of this "forced leisure." I learned that, in good times or in times of challenge, getting sucked into the power of things that are less relevant made me begin to lose sight of the treasures that matter the most.

Rich Thoughts

When have you been forced to pause with your thoughts, words, or actions?

_____

_____

_____

_____

_____

_____

_____

_____

_____

_____

_____

_____

_____

Rich Point for Your Day

Today I will remain still so as to recapture the necessities of life.

Life is RICH when you are able to acknowledge that . . .

Taking steps forward sometimes requires you to take two steps backwards.

This was our second property that we had purchased and to say the least we were very content with everything it had to offer. Our new dwelling was in close proximity of our son's school and was close to relatives, the grocery store, and so much more. This place was a home filled with love and happiness and continued to be even after our home had flooded. The dealings with the property manager and everything thereafter at that time appeared to have been a setback, not knowing that the benefits that we would be reaping would only propel us forward.

It happened so fast, water spewing everywhere and all over our wooden floors and the house's contents. However, although many of our items became submerged in water, everything remained intact. It was only the people that lived beneath us and the occupants who lived the floor under them that had some minor water damage. All in all, everything appeared to be well until the property manager said otherwise. At first in accordance to her, it was not our fault and would fall on the shoulders of the condo corporation, and then it became our problem. To make matters worse, we had no content insurance. For with the hustle and bustle of the move into our home, it seemed that that had literally flown over our heads, and now we were required to take some steps backward.

Backward in the sense that we were now beginning to see that, although our home was our sweet and safe haven, there were so many other issues that needed to be rightfully addressed concerning the condo corporation. So we made the big decision to place our condo up for sale on the market, which needless to say sold within two days. And although we had in our minds as to a place where we wanted to live, we ended up living with family members for close to one whole year.

However, although it seemed as if we were constantly taking steps backward, it led us back to full circle and allowed us to take the necessary steps forward in finding ourselves another home, which was even better than before.

Rich Thoughts

Back, back, forth, and forth. What connections can be made to you and your life when you hear those words?

_____

_____

_____

_____

_____

_____

_____

_____

_____

_____

_____

_____

Rich Point for Your Day

Today, I will realize that, although I may move backward, I WILL move forward.

Life is RICH when you are able to acknowledge that . . .

If you succeed, it gives others the opportunity to succeed.

I have assisted many students, whether they be in grade 8 and are transitioning into their high school of choice or adults who are shadowing me as their host teacher, having a hand in the ability to be instrumental with their journeys by allowing them to have the opportunity to showcase their talents, and then finding out that they have been accepted into a performing arts or a baccalaureate school or have landed a profession in education as a teacher is a very rewarding experience and tugs at my heart.

I had received a message from a friend and colleague that one of my former students (who was a third year university student at that time) had come back to one of the schools where I had been employed, to assist her with the school musical. My friend continued to write how much she missed me and how the students were doing. As I continued to read the message via my iPhone, tears began to well up in my eyes because of the kind words that I continued to read. The message spoke about how instrumental my teaching methods were, and because of my willingness and mission for others to succeed, this former student wrote that now she succeeds and lives by my classroom motto at that time: "A journey of a thousand miles begins with a single step."

I was so moved by her written words and how sharp her memory in remembering this Chinese proverb. She said that she literally applied this proverb to her daily life, furthermore thanking me for all I had done for her and her fellow classmates at that time, despite the fact when I was prepping them for the future, they were resistant to it. For what we do not realize is how powerful and instrumental educators are in either making or breaking a student's spirit or passion to learn. We can breathe either life or death into their lives on an academic or personal level. I chose my words, actions, and thoughts to breathe and mirror life. For all I ever wanted for those who were placed in my life was to succeed.

Rich Thoughts

Think of a time when you have helped someone else to succeed at what they set out to do. How did that make you feel?

_____

_____

_____

_____

_____

_____

_____

_____

_____

_____

_____

_____

_____

Rich Point for Your Day

Today I will remember that, when I help others to succeed, I have succeeded as well.

Life is RICH when you are able to acknowledge that . . .

Two wrongs don't make a right.

A wrongful action is not a morally appropriate way to correct or cancel a previous wrongful action, so when someone has dished out to you a great amount of dirt, what do you do? Do you fight fire with fire? Or do you turn the other cheek and proceed to passively look the other way? This scenario tended to be my situation in high school, at least for a minute, and although I knew that two wrongs did not make things right, I was always taught that it was never right to wrong someone even if they have wronged you first, because their wrong plus your wrong together would not necessarily make a right situation. I found that I made excuses to be right, and the teachings reiterated to me by my parents went in one ear and out the next.

High school was a fascinating time for me. Not only was I an exceptional student, I was also quite the athlete. Balancing my academics, sports, hanging out with my friends, and being miss social butterfly, not to mention maintaining my personal life and my family life, was not difficult for me to do. It was rather the opposite; it was all quite easy for me.

I loved school and everything about it, and I was quite proud that the only time I visited the office was to either sign in or out of school for an appointment. So when the principal called into one of my classes and said that she wanted to see me in her office, I all but crapped myself with an eagerness of anticipating the unknown. Rumor had it that the principal was thinking of suspending me. Now when I heard that, I became infuriated because I knew that it had something to do with what had transpired in the hallway a little earlier on that afternoon. I know that I did not initiate the *little altercation* that happened in the crowded hallway.

But instead of getting terribly upset, I only walked in with butterflies in my stomach. I explained to the principal that two female students and I had brushed shoulders—actually, to be exact, one of the female students bumped into me and then said to me, "Watch where you're going." At that point I said to her with attitude, "YOU watch where you are going you . . ." At that point she said she was going to go to the principal with what just took place to tell her that I harassed her. My response was "Go right ahead."

After the principal listened some more, she calmly replied "You know that two wrongs don't make a right" and proceeded to say that it was only because I was a great student and athlete that deterred her from suspending me. As I sat in the chair adjacent of her desk, I held a silent prayer of gratitude because only God knows that my parents would not have been happy to learn of this. I also replied to my principal that I do know better and allowed the best of that girl to get to me, when in fact I should have kept my cool.

That day was just a little reminder to what my parents had instilled in me from a young age—that what monkey sows, the monkey should not always do.

Rich Thoughts

Has someone ever wronged you? If so, how did that make you feel?

_____

_____

_____

_____

_____

_____

_____

_____

_____

_____

_____

_____

_____

Rich Point for Your Day

Today I will remember just because someone has done something to me that I did not like, it doesn't make it right for me to participate in the same wrongdoing. I will be the better person.

Life is RICH when you are able to acknowledge that . . .

Freedom allows you to play freely.

I have observed that, when children play, they become totally oblivious to anything and everything that goes on around them. At times I have earnestly questioned their ability to hear. Can they seriously not hear you, or are they also playing their own game, the game they know all too well—the selective hearing game. However, upon observing children's play and their demeanor a bit more closely, it became quite evident that their lack of hearing was associated with and only with their ability to be free—free from having to hear any adult voices, and more importantly, free from the expectation of having to follow instructions. I believe excited them even more because they are able to be themselves.

For children to be free to imagine, create, and then make-believe in their play world allows them to venture into another world. Within this particular world, the power or right to act, speak, or think as children want to think without a hint of hindrance or restraint makes playing more enjoyable.

It was the evening before my birthday, and I had planned an evening with the girls, an evening filled with all the things that I liked to play with, was going to be on the venue. I was hosting a pole dance birthday party, then we were going to go out to eat and be merry. I had wanted to take part in pole dancing exercise classes before because I had found it extremely fascinating to watch how the women would work the pole. Wrapping, twisting, turning, and spinning around a pole—I found it all to look sexy. But because of health issues, I was unable to do so. So when my health became better, I could not wait to play and be free to do the *unthinkable*. I was going to imagine, create, and make-believe some more that I was an exotic dancer.

We listened to the given instructions and then tried to follow the lead of our multitalented instructor. We were able to do most of the moves, however, to the beat of our own drum and giggled every now and then and sometimes gave our instructor that side eye only because she did everything so effortlessly.

Having this time with my girls to act in a manner much like how children do and having the opportunity to be free of our wife or mommy duties, even if it was for a few hours, made our time together even more enjoyable.

Rich Thoughts

In your own words, define the concept *freedom*.

_____

_____

_____

_____

_____

_____

_____

_____

_____

_____

_____

_____

Rich Point for Your Day

Today I will be carefree with myself.

Life is RICH when you are able to acknowledge that . . .

Money can't buy you love or happiness.

I remember reading a particular news article whose title captured my attention. It was about a billionaire who ended up taking his own life. Normally I would not even entertain myself in reading such a negative newspaper article; however, this one seemed to have piqued my interest enough to allow me to continue on.

I recollect feeling very badly for this individual who for some unknown reason felt that it would be better to commit suicide rather than find solace in a family member, friend, or our Heavenly Father during his time of despair.

As tough as life may appear to be, despite the tests, trials, and tribulations that endlessly surface and resurface on a daily basis, I still find it baffling as to why a person would risk everything and hurt others in the process of doing so. Was this billionaire's life that dismal, completely void of love and happiness?

In accordance with most societies and communities in the world, this man had everything, didn't he? However, as I continued to read more of this article, I learned that this billionaire was experiencing financial turmoil that affected his businesses and had furthermore trickled into every area of this man's life.

The article that I did not want to initially read turned out to teach a valuable lesson. Although this billionaire appeared to have everything, he literally had nothing, for money could not buy this man love or happiness. It appeared that the billionaire's acquisition of wealth and title attached to his name defined who he was, and although it would appear to the general public, his business partners, and so forth that he had it all, it was the complete opposite. He became broken and felt alone and lost, and his empire became broken. It is so unfortunate that we look to money to fill the void of happiness. Yes, we require money to live a certain lifestyle and to acquire the good things in life. I am a living example of this. I know what it is to make, and I know what it is not to make. But I will say this that money can't buy you love or happiness.

Rich Thoughts

Do you think that by having more money would allow you to feel happy? Explain your thoughts.

_____

_____

_____

_____

_____

_____

_____

_____

_____

_____

_____

_____

_____

Rich Point for Your Day

Today I will remember that money is important but not as important as love and happiness.

Life is RICH when you are able to acknowledge that . . .

Lessons are to be learned and never to be forgotten

Life is such a special occasion that is filled with so many memorable lessons. Although many of the lessons presented to you in your lifespan may not be to your liking and you vow that they are not worth remembering, these neatly packaged gifts are still lessons that should never be forgotten. For if we were to forget them, how would we ever really learn or equip ourselves with the knowledge that we now know for betterment?

My husband and I had decided to have lunch at a local restaurant, and in doing so, I believe that we both left with a newfound appreciation for the word *lesson*.

I noticed a man seated behind us, but I did not think anything of it. We began eating, then the same man seated behind us was now standing adjacent to the table where we were seated. He appeared to look *normal*, but when he spoke, it appeared as if his current situation was anything but that.

What I found rather interesting is that, unlike the other individuals who approach you for money, he did the opposite. He asked if we would buy him a bus token. My husband pulled out his wallet without hesitation and gave him some money instead. I asked him if it was really what he had asked us for, and he replied yes as the tears began to well up in his eyes. He continued to answer my questions and said that he was most grateful and had watched us come into the restaurant as he sat—at that time under a tree. He said that day so many people heard his plea for help, yet they did not attend to his cries of desperation. He explained to us that, that very morning, he was evicted from his home and that his estranged wife moved to an undisclosed area, and he has custody of their two daughters.

My heart dropped for I know what it was to have and to not have money and also that what life has to offer us is not what we intended it to be. At that point my husband asked him if he wanted some of our food. We had not touched or even eaten any at this point. I observed his hesitation, so I encouraged him to take it. I gave him a bottle of water and continued to listen as he spoke from a place of destitute and despair.

His two daughters were with a neighbor, and as we listened some more, we were relieved that he didn't make the choice to go a shelter but decided to go to his mother. As he was leaving, I asked him if it would be okay for us to pray with him. He accepted. We encouraged him to not let go of the light of God. We gave him a few more dollars and saw him off his way.

All this transpired in a restaurant. A man felt compelled to seek us out, we chose to listen, unlike the many others who silenced his voice and turned a blind eye to his cries.

That day I relearned an invaluable lesson that we must always do good to others as we would want others do unto us. We should not judge and should lean more to helping those in need and more importantly do this with a willing heart.

Rich Thoughts

What lessons have you learned?

_____
_____
_____
_____
_____
_____
_____
_____
_____
_____
_____
_____

Rich Point for Your Day

Today I will remember that learning is an ongoing process.

Life is RICH when you are able to acknowledge that . . .

Time left alone in the wilderness reveals truth.

At first we thought that our son's inability to walk without falling down was due to growing pains. However, when these growing pains episode continued to happen to our son, we began questioning its purpose and quickly made an appointment with our family physician. It was only after having seen a physiatrist, receiving an x-ray and an MRI for his left knee, and two referrals to orthopedic surgeons that we were made aware of his condition. Apparently he had a lesion on his joint on the left knee. Having said that, he became under strict orders to not participate in any physical or sports-related activities for ten months.

In the months to come, what had transpired required a time of questions that ultimately revealed truth in the end not only to our son but to us all. When left alone in an uncultivated region, the truth unraveled.

It would be difficult for an adult much less a child to experience not being able to participate in any sports-related or physical activities from October up until August. It was very difficult to see our child not to do the things that he enjoyed doing and to explain to him the importance of staying low so that what needs to be healed can be healed. But despite having felt that way, as parents we always taught him about believing with persistence that all would be well. Our son went deep within himself and visited a place that was foreign to him. Here he abandoned his dreams of ever being able to participate in sports and neglected the other things that were of importance to him. This was very difficult to see especially because before he was such an active boy who did everything and anything! However, during these times of difficulty, so much was revealed to our son. Firstly, patience is required in all that we do, for being in the wilderness required him to listen and to interpret what he heard, and the massages and acupuncture were indeed working to his benefit. He said that he was able to spend more time with his Creator and to see that all things do work for his betterment. He said that, because he had all those months and time to think and to be left alone with his thoughts regarding what was taking place with his health, the wilderness revealed truth that all he had to do was to trust and believe that all would be well.

Rich Thoughts

Name a time when you had to venture into the wilderness. What happened?

_____

_____

_____

_____

_____

_____

_____

_____

_____

_____

_____

_____

Rich Point for Your Day

Today I will be accepting of what the wilderness has to offer.

Life is RICH when you are able to acknowledge that . . .

Shutting out every voice and sound is the greatest gift of mindfulness.

To shut out means to bar or no longer allow, and normally when I feel as if my world is closing in on me, I remove myself rather quickly from that world of confusion.

While others may indulge in eating chocolate, drinking alcohol, or experimenting with drugs, I chose to walk. My walks may be for a short period of time or a longer period of time. However, whenever I go on my walking escapades, my mind usually would become clearer and block out each voice and sound that may have caused me grief a few minutes before. These thoughts would then dissipate and blend into the background of what I encountered within my surroundings.

I am learning that my walks are one of the greatest gifts to practice mindfulness, and I didn't realize how great it was until after having completed a chronic pain mindfulness mediation course last year. I practiced many kinds of mindfulness activities and exercises, and upon completion of meditation, everything seemed much clearer than what it was a few seconds before. My breathing would become regulated, and I would focus on the tasks at hand and then ultimately become one with myself, nature, and my Creator. So when things became overwhelming for me, I put on my shoes and walked.

Normally, I would begin to feel a bit of discomfort when I would participate in longer-than-expected walks, but with each step, I found that I became more empowered than the last and I found that I took note and became more observant of the scents, people, nature, and myself. Silence was golden and even more golden when I did not talk but just walked and appreciated the birds chirping, the slight breeze blowing in my hair, and the noise of the traffic or children in the park.

These moments allowed me to reflect and to think about my thinking of the things that were upsetting to me. Once I had accomplished this, my thoughts mirrored my mindfulness and allowed me to see how meaningless it is to allow miniscule things to bother me. The importance of shutting out every voice and sound in order to be mindful, positive, and productive is a must.

Rich Thoughts

Name some of the things that are a must for you to shut out in order for you to experience mindfulness.

_____

_____

_____

_____

_____

_____

_____

_____

_____

_____

_____

_____

Rich Point for Your Day

Today I will focus on the sound of my voice.

Life is RICH when you are able to acknowledge that . . .

You should not try to pray the storm away.

I am known to have paper surrounding me at all times, whether it is in the format of books, articles, poems, magazines, quotes, or writings of my own. I am always circled by knowledge and inspirational literature. When I was sorting through one of the small storage boxes that I have, one was filled with various items. Continuing on with my search, I came across a piece of paper that appeared to have been cut with scissors. Within the parameters of this piece of paper, the words *hope, renew,* and *strength* became the theme. I do not remember where this piece of paper came from or who had given it to me. What I do recall is that the thoughts were the most fitting for my circumstances and positioning in life and therefore thought it would be most beneficial to share with the world. It reads as follows:

When the storm hits, it sets its wings so that the wind will pick it up and lift it above the storm. While the storm rages below, the eagle is soaring above it. The eagle does not escape the storm. It rises on the winds that brings the storm.

When the storms of life come upon us (and all of us will experience them) we can rise above them by setting our minds and our belief toward God. The storms do not have to overcome us. We can allow God's power to lift us above them. God enables us to ride the winds of the storms that bring sickness, tragedy, failure, and disappointment in our lives. We can soar above the storm. Remember, it is not the burdens of life that weigh us down, it is how we handle those burdens.

As I read these thoughts that I found on that piece of paper, it allowed me to understand the importance of wanting not to eradicate or pray the actual storm away but to use the storm, as my father had shared with me one day, as a tool to educate, to learn, and ultimately to enable others to be lifted to higher heights. This is what I intend to do with my storms.

Rich Thoughts

What storms have you experienced lately?

_____
_____
_____
_____
_____
_____
_____
_____
_____
_____
_____
_____
_____

Rich Point for Your Day

Today I will pray until something happens, which will allow me to lean into the wind more acceptingly.

Life is RICH when you are able to acknowledge that . . .

Opportunity swings on the doors of dreams.

Who says that parks are just for children? Ha! Whoever thinks that statement to be true does not know what they are talking about and what they are truly missing. For being able to swing and then coast while being suspended in midair is truly an exhilarating experience.

When I was younger, I would frequent the park daily and would make it my duty to *try* every park apparatus in sight. It was fun to be able to meet up with your friends and just play, unlike the children today, who would rather play with their PS3s, Xbox ones, Wiis, and any other gadgets associated with technology within the beloved *world* of social media.

I still enjoy frequenting the parks to this day. I may not go on all the park apparatuses, but I will never abandon my love for using the swing. That love began with my father and our daily rendezvous' we had at the park as father and child. He would push me on the swings while he spoke about his dreams for me and the importance of allowing oneself to be free. I loved everything—the freedom, the unspeakable heights, and the ability to dream the unthinkable dream.

In July 2014 I had been invited to another women's red carpet social networking event. To say the least, I was rather excited to be an attendee, for having the opportunity to have been able to meet up with other women all under one roof in a positive and productive environment that had similar visions and goals was an awesome experience! This event reminded me very much of the parks I frequented as a child. Although there were no slides or climbing or spinning apparatuses, the women who congregated in that upscale hall all came for the same cause—to inspire, learn, and believe. We were ready to have fun, to meet up with other women, to listen to their plight, and to learn how they used their struggles to become successful women entrepreneurs. In doing so, it was very much like a park, where greatness boiled and bubbled.

The highlight of the evening for me was the networking aspect and also being able to listen to the other women's stories. I have made some solid business relationships that have blossomed into beautiful friendships. And with each story that was revealed that evening, I found a piece of me in every one of the women's testimonies. When they spoke, I was able to make connections to their experiences that made it that more real for me. Listening to them gave me the subtle confirmations of the things I had envisioned. I wanted my once-silenced dialogue to no longer be silenced. I wanted the programs and workshops that I created to reach other women. And having gone to this women's networking event allowed the doors of my dreams to be left ajar. And to say the least, I was excited!

I did not plan or intend on speaking at this event, much less in front of a crowd filled of women. However, the opportunity presented itself, and I gladly welcomed it. The event planner had three women on stage, each holding a small placard. The first read *POWERFUL,* the second *FIERCE*, and the last *STRENGTH*. We were instructed to choose one, and a few were invited to share their reasons as to why they chose that one word to describe themselves. I automatically associated with the concept strength and found myself raising my hand to volunteer my thoughts with the other women in attendance of this event.

That is when I was invited to swing on the swing of opportunity. I shared with these beautiful sisters how I was silenced by the daily liberties of life and how I chose to believe that I would succeed and what I did to propel forward in seeing these dreams become a reality. Because of the doors of the women of the red carpet networking event that I attended that evening, my opportunities of seeing Rich Chicks and all my other dreams associated with it come into fruition. I have swung on the swing of opportunity.

Rich Thoughts

List some of the opportunities that allowed your dreams to manifest.

_____

_____

_____

_____

_____

_____

_____

_____

_____

_____

_____

_____

_____

Rich Point for Your Day

Today I will swing as high as I can so as to nurture my dreams.

Life is RICH when you are able to acknowledge that . . .

You can win the championship.

Competitors are tenacious in their efforts to win. The first-place winner receives a prize of some sort, whether it is a trophy, medal, or ribbon. The winner receives a prize. But what happens when the race does not look as bright as you intended it to be?

The last time that I entered any form of track and field events was my last year of high school. Although very talented in the running and pit events, I chose to focus on my academic studies in university as opposed to committing all of my time training for track. It was just a couple of years ago that my son was participating at a track meet on the grounds of York University.

The interesting thing attending this particular meet was that it was really intended to be a track meet for youths. However, our children's coach entered some of the parents to run the 4 x 100 meters. This brought back so many amazing memories of everything associated with my former high school track meets. However, there is always so much more than what one sees. The runners winning their heats and their finals brought a smile to my face, but what others did not see was the hard work they had to put in for their winnings, and because it had obviously been some time that I had ran, that meant that not only did I have to attend the track practices, it also meant that I had to prepare myself not only physically but also mentally to win!

The book that you read was not intended to manifest into a published reading piece, yet here we are. You all as the readers or audience and I as the author. I commenced as a competitor in the race of life in both the track and in the field events. However, lately I had not been receiving first-, second-, or third-place medals but only participatory ribbons. To say the least, I was not used to receiving ribbons but very much used to getting gold and silver medals and the occasional bronze medal, plaques, and even some pictures and write-ups in the local newspaper. Life became too unpredictable, and thus when entering these events, I found that I became less motivated to carry on with the things that would normally not trouble me at all.

The women's/parents' 4 x 100 meters reminded me of these unpredictable events associated with track and field meets. We practiced during the week by stretching, jogging, doing our As, Bs, and Cs, and warm-ups. To say the least, we were determined to win this championship. However, when the announcer fired the starting gun, our first runner was nowhere to be found. Everyone had left her and the second runner was not doing that much better. However, when the baton arrived at the third exchange, the third runner began to lessen the gap between the other competitors, then when the baton arrived at the fourth exchange to where I was stationed, I grabbed that baton and gave it my all. What an amazing experience it was. I felt as if I were back in high school when I would do the same—bring the team to victory. As I listened to the cheers of the crowd in the stadium, it was a clear indication that they were just as elated as I was. Crossing that finish line was the best thing that I had done in a long time for it came during a time when a lot of self-doubt had unwillingly introduced itself to my life. When I crossed that finish line, I remember silently uttering, "I still have it . . . I still run a good race." That afternoon remains to be symbolic to my life in regards to the characteristics of that of a winner. Life is like a bowl of cherries, some sweet and some sour, and during those sour times, I chose to press on and fight for what was rightfully mine. I stretched and I practiced and dedicated all my time and effort to be the best that I could be in regaining back the true me. Although in my life I was faced with some hurdles, I did everything that I could possibly think of to win the championship of life.

Rich Thoughts

Have you ever won a championship? If yes, share your thoughts using a few phrases. If no, what championship do you wish you could have won?

_____

_____

_____

_____

_____

_____

_____

_____

_____

_____

_____

_____

_____

Rich Point for Your Day

Today I will remember that, even if I am not able to get that gold medal in anything that I have set out to accomplish, I still have won the championship.

Life is RICH when you are able to acknowledge that . . .

The best and most beautiful things in the world cannot be seen or even touched. They must be felt by the heart.
—Helen Keller

According to *Bing Dictionary* the heart is "the source of emotional life, where the deepest and most sincerest feelings are located."

When I think of the things that are most beautiful in life, it is a given that I think of the love I have for my husband, my son, family members, and genuine friends. I also think of how beautiful it is to experience inner peace. However, my love list is endless, but one other thing that I absolutely love is music and of course songs. Whenever I hear Alicia Keys's song "That's How Strong My Love Is," it literally takes my breath away and evokes a wealth of emotions—from sadness, frustration, and fear to joy, happiness, and love and expressions of new beginnings. This song allows me to feel the greatness of each rhythmic beat, each tempo, and each piano key that has been played. This beauty merges within my soul and sinks the depth of my heart. It reminds me of the love I have for my husband and how beautiful this love makes me feel. When I listen to or hear this song, it merges the beauty within and allows me to make connections with how beautiful it is to fall in love. It also reminds me of the woman that I am supposed to be for the betterment of my husband and how we sifted through the storms. But more importantly the most beautiful thing is that it is a reminder of the unbreakable bond and love we have for each other that is forever felt within our hearts.

Rich Thoughts

What was the most beautiful *thing* that ever happened to you? Choose just one.

_____

_____

_____

_____

_____

_____

_____

_____

_____

_____

_____

_____

Rich Point for Your Day

Today I will speak and feel with my heart.

Life is RICH when you are able to acknowledge that . . .

Swearing illustrates how limited your vocabulary really is.

I think that it was around high school when I realized that I had a potty mouth. I would swear for absolutely nothing at all. If I was frustrated or upset or if something fell from me, I would swear. If someone got me extremely irate, if I was going to be late for an event, if I missed the bus or an important call, or if I was hungry or at a loss for words, I would swear.

Mind you, I know better and dare not utter or expel these profane and obscene words from my mouth in front of my parents. That would definitely be a disaster and an absolute big no-no.

Not only was it a distasteful habit that I had picked up, it was also a blessing in disguise in a weird kind of way. On one hand, it could sound mildly or highly offensive to one's ear, while on the other hand, swearing became an emotional outlet and relieved me from the stress and tension presented in my life.

However, as I got older, I began to learn that, although unexpected things may happen—like stubbing my toe on the edge of the bed frame while trying to find my way from the washroom back to the bed in the dark or slamming my finger in a drawer—I knew that there would be another outlet that would not warrant such a limited expression of offensive words. So each day I worked at limiting my newfound habit. I had to unlearn these new forms of expressions because they hindered my true ability to truly speak. I personally believe that, when a person swears as much as I used to, it points a finger to how limited one's vocabulary is. Because one cannot find the appropriate words to express oneself, they are substituted with a word that really bears no meaning. So yes, I used to participate in using swearwords sometimes either to evoke a specific reaction from others or to express frustration or surprise. But along with maturity came the need to wise up and pay attention to how offensive it made me look and how offensive it was to others.

Rich Thoughts

When was the first time that you had sworn?

_____
_____
_____
_____
_____
_____
_____
_____
_____
_____
_____
_____
_____

Rich Point for Your Day

Today I will remember that, when I swear, I do myself an injustice to my intelligence.

Life is RICH when you are able to acknowledge that . . .

Infinite love evokes new thoughts of expression.

Today I didn't feel to drive or to be driven, nor did I want anyone to keep me company for that matter. I wanted to go to my destination solo, and I ended up doing so by taking the local transit system. When I got onto the bus, a woman who was a mother of two sat two seats away from where I was seated. As I watched her fuss over her daughter and her son, I watched her constantly kiss and hug them both. She would fix her daughter's hair and attend to the needs of her physically challenged son. This reminded me of the love that I have for my child.

However, I was noticing that, despite the intimate love I have for my son, it seemed as if at times the mother-child relationship that we both were familiar with was left on pause, and this left me feeling sad.

I am aware that when children hit puberty and become teenagers, they seek their own identity and are in search for their own independence, where they want to think and do things for themselves. Furthermore, there are struggles and challenges of what will be. I am also aware that, during these stages of their lives, they tend to pull away from their parents. But these mood swings and the staying in the room and speaking only when wanting to engage in conversations of his choice were a bit much for me to swallow. He will always be my baby regardless of the fact that my son is embarking on a new journey and taking a new path to manhood.

For the rest of the bus ride, I continued watching this mother and her two children. I did not mind if people questioned my motives for looking at them with warm smiles. For that is how they made me feel to see them express their endless love for one another. What I saw was impossible to measure or calculate, and it allowed me to truly reflect on how much I missed that kind of relationship with my son. It was also brought to my conscious mind that, as a mother, I am to always fulfill my duty.

It only dawned on me then that I have and will always continue to love him unconditionally just as this mother did for her children, particularly her disabled son. She took him out of the stroller and placed her son beside me. As the bus swayed to and fro, so did he, and in doing so, he landed on me. Other times when the bus was not in motion, he chose to lean his head on my shoulder. Strangely enough I allowed him. His innocence was pure. Other times he reached for my cell and other times had a fascination for the curls in my hair. What happened on the bus touched me greatly. For it also reminded me that no matter what I must continue to pick my child up when he talks and make sure that he is all right every step of the way while partaking in his journey. When life allows our son to sway to and fro, I will continue to be there. But more importantly, I will continue to make known my thoughts and feelings for him by infusing in my son the infinite love I will forever have for him.

Rich Thoughts

What does the word *infinite* mean to you?

_____

_____

_____

_____

_____

_____

_____

_____

_____

_____

_____

_____

Rich Point for Your Day

Today I will let my love create new thoughts.

Life is RICH when you are able to acknowledge that . . .

I AM proud to be myself, flaws and all.

I think I was in grade 6 when I approached my mother and told her that I wanted to have a bum operation to reduce the size. When my mother heard this, she didn't display any signs of anger but instead responded in a calm manner and had asked me why I would want to do such a thing.

My response was that I thought that my behind was too big and therefore wanted it to be a bit smaller so that I would not be teased by some of the boys that attended my elementary school. This was the point when my mother had a heartfelt talk with me about accepting myself for who I am. This mother-daughter talk was most needed and set me down the path of self-acceptance and self-love, for I continued to constantly love myself—every inch and ounce of ME.

Looking back at that incident, I am now in a place that allows me to laugh, but more importantly it has allowed me to be diligent in my quest to ensure that other females also accept themselves for who they are, no matter the circumstance.

We live in a society where *others* dictate and define what beauty is. From this message, there are girls, young adults, and women who are walking around believing that they are not good enough, pretty enough, or smart enough because they do not fit into societal perception of what beauty truly is.

Although I was raised to be proud of my ethnicity and myself, there was a point in time when I doubted what my parents had instilled in me because of a group of jerks who saw it fit to make fun of my behind. Thank God for my parents and thank God for my mother, who allowed me to embrace my *imperfections.* I believe that is why, when I became an educator, I created a girls discussion group that catered to the issues that revolve around the daily concerns or struggles that young females face. I gave them an outlet and an opportunity for them to hear stories, attend lectures and workshops, and participate in activities that equipped them with the tools of acceptance and self-love in order to gain back their voices and eradicate the silenced dialogues that became so familiar to them.

Because of that one incident, it empowered me to make it my duty to allow others to embrace and celebrate their uniqueness. Today I continue to do that with my business Rich Chicks for women who yearn to be refreshed, renewed, and restored. I give them the tools to equip themselves so that their inward treasures are rediscovered, and in doing so, with every imperfection related to self that was revealed now becomes a distant memory, and it transformed the woman into a more accepting and a more forgiving person where she can now feel comfortable and proud of who she is.

Rich Thoughts

Make a short list consisting of a few words of some of the things that you are most proud about YOURSELF.

_____

_____

_____

_____

_____

_____

_____

_____

_____

_____

_____

_____

_____

Rich Point for Your Day

Today I will embrace my imperfections. I remain to be proud of MYSELF.

Life is RICH when you are able to acknowledge that . . .

Sometimes you have to gently brush away the cobwebs of yesterdays.

We had accompanied a family member to the doctor's office, and while waiting for them to complete an ultrasound, I sighted a pregnant woman and her partner. I smiled at them both and watched the woman waddle toward her destination, while her partner walked proudly behind her. I assumed that the lab technician would be giving them their first or maybe second ultrasound readings. Perhaps they would be finding out the sex of their child. I found myself intrigued with this couple and observed them intently. When they were leaving the office, they both seemed pleased with whatever results they were told. And I began to become engulfed with a sea of emotions as I entertained the thought of what was no longer my reality.

This was the first time that I had ever responded in such a manner. I have seen numerous couples before who were expecting a child. However, that morning my mind began to wander back to my most recent miscarriage. It became so overwhelming to even see the information that was posted on the wall pertaining to the different stages of one's baby's development. As I glanced on, I read that you were given the option of capturing and enjoying these precious moments with the latest 3-D technology. That is when the tears began to fall, and I excused myself and told my husband that I would be back in a minute. He was unaware of what was going on until he asked me if everything was okay. At that point he saw the distress displayed on my face and proceeded to lead me out of the doctor's office.

Without me even having to say a single word, he seemed to have understood. As I turned away from him and the people that were now flooding the hallway, the tears seemed to have flowed even more than before. He held me and allowed me to go through the motions, so to speak, until those feelings subsided and then came to a halt.

Who would have ever thought that the cobwebs of yesterday would still be there. I was not a bitter person toward those who carried their babies to term, nor did I harbor ill feelings or thoughts toward couples that I have seen in public places. But for some unknown reason, that day caused me to cave in. And when I caved in to these feelings that were buried for so long, it showed me the importance of making sure that I make it my duty to gently brush away the cobwebs of yesterday so that today may be filled with webs of joy and happiness.

I will never forget how blessed I have been to experience life growing inside of me, nor will I forget the dark moments when we learned that a heartbeat could not be detected. Both moments, despite how uncomfortable or how angry they made me feel, were required in order to truly heal. Addressing those cobwebs is now much easier to do. I do not shed as many tears as I once did. But I have come to the realization that, because of my experiences, I am able to comfort those who have gone or who are going through something quite similar to my plight, and that in itself is worth it.

Rich Thoughts

What cobwebs tend to reappear in your life? What steps were required in order to get rid of them?

_____

_____

_____

_____

_____

_____

_____

_____

_____

_____

_____

_____

Rich Point for Your Day

Today I will face the cobwebs of my world boldly and continuously brush them away until they are no longer in existence.

Life is RICH when you are able to acknowledge that . . .

Time is NOT guaranteed.

I remember reading an inspirational short story that I saw posted on my friend's timeline on Facebook. It spoke about the relationship between a father and his son. The son had asked his father how much he made in an hour, and although his father's response was that it was none of his son's concern, he ended up caving in and telling his son that he made one hundred dollars per hour. The son seemed thrilled to learn how much his father had earned at an hourly rate and proceeded to ask him if he could borrow fifty dollars.

His father was not pleased with this and told his son that he will not tolerate such childish behavior and that he works to hard for his money. His response was substantiated in believing that his son had only wanted the money to purchase a silly toy.

After some time had elapsed the father began to think that perhaps his son had really needed to purchase something, because he rarely asked him for money. The father decided to see if his son was asleep, only to find out that he was awake. The father and son spoke about what had taken place, and the father apologized for being too harsh with him and ended up giving his son the fifty-dollar bill.

The little boy began to smile and begun to take out some of his other money that he had placed crumpled up underneath the pillow. When his father saw this, he began to get cross again. However, the little boy continued to slowly count his money. The father continued to ask his son why he would want more money if he knew that he had money all along. The son responded to his father that he did not have enough money before, but now that his father has given him the fifty-dollar bill, he had more than enough. The man's son now had one hundred dollars and wanted to know if he could buy an hour of his father's time.

When I read what the little boy had set out to accomplish with his father, my heart sank and literally skipped a beat. As I continued reading further, I got to learn that with this one-hundred-dollar bill the little boy had saved up, all he wanted to do was have dinner with his father. When his father heard this, he too felt crushed and begged for his son's forgiveness.

This story has allowed me to reflect upon the relationship I have with my loved ones and how important it is to challenge ourselves and be aware of how we spend that time with the people who matter to us the most and who are close to our hearts. I learned that we should never let time slip through our fingers to the point in which this father had done. We should not live to work but work to live, for time is not guaranteed.

Rich Thoughts

When have you wished for there to be more time in the day?

_____
_____
_____
_____
_____
_____
_____
_____
_____
_____
_____
_____
_____

Rich Point for Your Day

Today I will share my time with the people that I love.

Life is RICH when you are able to acknowledge that . . .

The highest stilettos can be your best friend.

I believe the first time that I ever owned my own pair of heels was when I was seven years old. And although they were only *kitty heels*, I wore them well. As I got older, the inches to my heels got longer and each year I graduated from the school of heels until I became an adult and received my diploma or certification within the special area of the wearing of the ultimate heels—the stilettos. And to say the least, I was quite proud in receiving this title because what fashionista wouldn't?

There is something about owning a pair of stilettos that screams confidence and sexy to me. At one point I thought that I would possibly require therapy for the purchasing of these kinds of shoes, for I owned many of them. I absolutely loved everything about them—the way that they added height and accentuated and elongated my legs, how they changed my posture and made me walk tall—but most of all I LOVED how the stilettos allowed me to feel like I was a big-time celebrity walking down the red carpet. That is when the love affair with stilettos became known to everyone.

Even when I was pregnant with my son, I still refused to shelf these beauties and continued to walk the walk without causing any harm to my unborn child or myself. However, there was a point in time when I had no other choice but to sever all ties with my best friend, the stilettos, due to chronic lower and middle back pain and other ailments associated with my motor vehicle accident. And as a result, I was forced to wear flats and sneakers. How boring could one get? Interestingly enough these shoe transition days stretched out to months and then years, and during these times I looked at my stilettos that I once wore that were situated in my closet. Looking back at not being able to wear these bad boys symbolically represented that I no longer had the self-confidence that I once did, nor did I attend any functions that in the past allowed me to strut my stuff and walk in a more feminine way. Due to everything associated with the aftermath of the motor vehicle accident, my physical, emotional, and spiritual well-being became altered, which also affected my love affair with the stilettos. I became broken for a long while, and having to wear flats and sneakers illustrated the way I felt. However, with time my best friend began to resurface here and there, and I slowly rekindled the friendship as it was before, and in doing so, I was able to strut once more the things my best friend gave me.

Rich Thoughts

Describe your favorite pair of shoes. What do you like most about them?

_____

_____

_____

_____

_____

_____

_____

_____

_____

_____

_____

_____

_____

Rich Point for Your Day

Today I will strut with my best friend—my highest stilettos—and have some girls' fun.

Life is RICH when you are able to acknowledge that . . .

The mirror is not the enemy.

There are many reasons as to why people do not like to look in the mirror. It may be that they have put on some weight, have a blemish on some part of their face, or are beginning to see the effects of the many sleepless nights they have encountered, which are now showing up as bags under their eyes. On the other hand, there are those individuals that clearly enjoy looking in the mirror and tend to do so several times for the day. Whether that be at home or in public, let's say, at the mall, I most definitely fit into the second category. I could look in a mirror for the entire day if you let me, and it's not because I am vain but because I wanted to make sure that everything looked perfect, from the crown of my head to the tip of my toes, because I wanted everything to remain that way even if deep down inside the things that people wished to see was totally different from what I saw.

I always had things in order and because of this, people also expected me to have them in order. My words mirrored that notion of greatness, along with my actions and thoughts too! So why was it that, when I looked in the mirror, the person I now saw was no longer a person who smiled back at me? When did these changes occur? I began to see the mirror as the enemy and no longer found the pleasure of seeing my reflection, which made absolutely no sense because to the naked eye all seemed well, but to my soul, my image began to reflect the things only on the surface. Things were most definitely changing. It took a long time for me to comprehend that I was not the enemy; it was my circumstances that allowed theses changes to commence. Being placed on a pedestal by family members and friends at a young age became the norm, and therefore that is all I became to know. Even when diagnosed with posttraumatic stress and depression, I continued to see greatness and someone smiling back at me despite having this illness, for when I looked in the mirror, I ignored what my eyes really saw because of my inability to accept that I had changed and was no longer the person who I used to see in that mirror for decades. So I avoided looking into my mirror until I came to grip with the harsh reality that it's okay not to have everything in order, that it's okay to fall apart, that it's okay to look tired and not have every strand of hair in place. And once I came to the realization that my voice now mirrored the words of acceptance, the mirror became a friend and no longer an enemy to me.

Rich Thoughts

What speech do your words mirror?

_____
_____
_____
_____
_____
_____
_____
_____
_____
_____
_____

Rich Point for Your Day

Today I will face the person I see in the mirror and commence to change my ways. Today my speech will mirror the words of acceptance.

Life is RICH when you are able to acknowledge that . . .

Strength is achieved through a willingness to surrender.

It had been four years since the last time that I saw my friends, colleagues, and the school in which I had taught. I had been avoiding coming there because I could. It was too painful to visit before, but this time I had no other choice but to come in and collect my teaching belongings that had been packed up and stored in my former principal's office since April 2010. When I received an e-mail from my former principal, I automatically went into panic mode because of what I had been avoiding for years. I finally declared myself defeated and succumbed to my persistent ways in not wanting to go. I relinquished my control as it related to this decision which was the hardest thing for me to do. However, it had been a long time coming. So I eagerly became complacent and took a seat.

I must have called a few times, and on the fourth try, I heard a familiar soft-spoken voice. When she heard mine, she paused for a moment and then spoke of how much I was missed and if I was okay. When I began to speak, my voice began to tremble and I became overwhelmed with my thoughts and words. It took us a moment, but then I replied to her question. She paged another teacher, I saw many other friends and colleagues, and exchanged hugs, smiles, and even tears. But with each action, word, or thought, the load I had been carrying for so long began to lighten as I heard my voice speak to and address each one's concerns. My dialogue was no longer silenced, and for the first time, I felt free. All the anxiety that was built up inside of me for the past week had left my mind, body, and spirit. I believed that when the boxes were loaded into the vehicle, when I said my last good-byes and gave my last smile, gave and received my last hugs, that is when I said to myself, "It is done." That is when I realized that I took that amount of years to prepare myself to freely give all of me and trust that ALL would be well once I surrendered all.

Rich Thoughts

Have you ever thrown in the towel and surrender to it all?

_____

_____

_____

_____

_____

_____

_____

_____

_____

_____

_____

_____

Rich Point for Your Day

Today I surrender in attempt to be more self-sufficient.

Life is RICH when you are able to acknowledge that . . .

Each day is a wonderful gift.

Who doesn't like to receive gifts? I know that I do and will continue liking to receive them. I still remember all the *special* occasions where gift giving are involved. Birthdays gifts, "just because" gifts, Mother's Day gifts, Valentine's gifts, "You are so hot" gifts, anniversary gifts, and of course, Christmas gifts. Don't get me wrong, all these special days should not have to include a gift, but it does make it that much more intriguing.

I had just finished submitting travel documentation to the passport office; that in itself was a gift because I had been searching frantically for my expired passport for almost three weeks now and had just found it miraculously a few nights before. I say this was a gift because I searched high and low and to no avail the location of my passport could not be found. So in celebration of me getting through, I decided that I had wanted to browse and possibly purchase some items for myself from a particular store. Most of the stores were not yet opened in the mall, so because it was quite early in the morning, I decided to take a seat on a bench that was situated right in front of *my* store and participated in watching some people. I observed many things that morning. There were couples, teenagers, employees, grandparents with their children, and a few other people seated around the vicinity to where I sat. I saw a young lady with blond hair and another young woman who was walking with her. For some reason, although I quickly took my eyes off them and continued on with my *watching*, a few minutes later, the same blonde haired woman approached me. She had wanted to know if I knew when the store was going to open. I told her that I believed that it would be 10:00 a.m. and also told her that I too was waiting for them to open. She said thank you and proceed to take a seat beside me while the other young woman stood close by. Not long after, a more mature couple had asked her if she knew the location of the passport office. She had replied no. I then reassured them that it was close by and gave them accurate directions to their destinations. They said thank you and then left.

The blonde haired woman said to me that it must be my day to help those in need. My response was "I think so." She continued to speak to me about her life-pressing issues and even began to shed some tears. This touched me in such a profound way that I began on this emotional roller coaster with the blonde haired woman. I guess because her plight was so real and furthermore because I could related, I felt compelled to share some of my story with her in hopes for her to know that this too shall pass and that she was not alone. We spoke more, and she began to tell me that she didn't know what it was about me, but she could see pure light encompassing me and said as if I were an angel of some sort. I was most humbled by her kind words. She continued to tell me that I have a special gift to help, and the way I had spoken to her had motivated her to appreciate and live each day as if they were special gifts. We hugged each other. I and this blonde haired woman, this complete stranger, shared a most special gift to each other. She willingly gave me verbal confirmation of what I needed to continue doing in my life. Her present to me was the self-realization of the importance of helping youth and women with the things that they may be struggling with.

That day was inspiringly delightful and had me feeling extremely good, knowing that each day is a gift that should be cherished wisely.

Rich Thoughts

What part of your day do you consider to be a gift to you?

_____
_____
_____
_____
_____
_____
_____
_____
_____
_____
_____
_____

Rich Point for Your Day

Today I shall remember that each day is a special gift. For the treasures that are rediscovered shows the beauty of each gem, hence each day is special.

Life is RICH when you are able to acknowledge that . . .

It ain't worth it.

Laughter and more importantly a smile are always two important things that I think everyone should always do more of. I find that in today's fast-paced society we have been fashioned in such a manner that embraces others to feel comfortable with worrying and to complain and complain some more. We have lost the ability and have become preoccupied with the other things deemed more important, rather than leaning on one's understanding of what it truly means to experience joy and happiness.

Worry less, smile more, don't regret, just learn and grown. These are the ingredients required for a life filled with laughter. In doing so, not only will this allow you to live a stress-free life but it will allow you to appreciate the unappreciated things in our lives and look at them with a fresh new pair of eyes and a new attitude.

All in all, it is not worth it to do anything that will ruffle your feathers because in the end it affects you and only you. I think I came to this realization when I became an adult, and although I still try and try some more to *get it right*, I am in a better place of understanding the true importance of not being bothered by nothing and to learn to say "It ain't worth it." And once you lean towards not regretting what has been done but to the learning aspect of growing from these things. Then you will become familiar with, believe and therefore act like *it ain't worth it*. Not in a manner that will cause you harm but will cause you to be free.

Laughter is the remedy for all illnesses that one may encounter in life. And although at times it may be hard to do, just remember it ain't worth it and let that be the start to your new journey of joy, happiness and loads of smiles.

Rich Thoughts

Think of a time, then write about when it absolutely was not worth it!

_____

_____

_____

_____

_____

_____

_____

_____

_____

_____

_____

_____

_____

Rich Point for Your Day

Today I will let whatever it is go and shout at the top of my lungs, "It ain't worth it!"

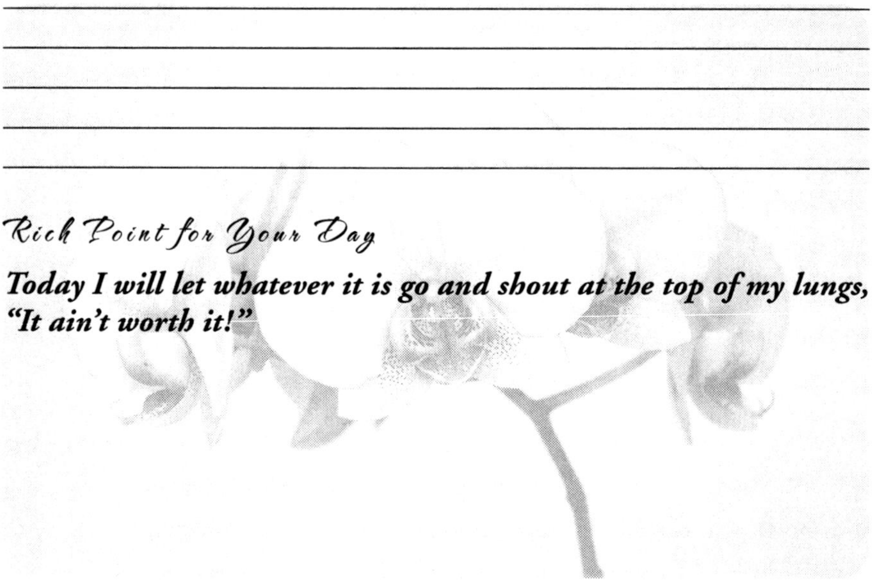

Life is RICH when you are able to acknowledge that . . .

It is well.

Five days before my son's first day as a grade 9 student at his new high school, and things seemed to be on the up-and-up. Today, however, was the grade 9 orientation, where he would be receiving a tour of the school, participate in activities, and partake in the eating of some barbequed food.

He asked if we, as his parents wanted to accompany him and attend part of his grade 9 orientation presentation. This seemed quite out of the ordinary for our son to ask, so we didn't question his motives and we agreed to accompany him. However, upon closer to the time, he opted to go by himself because he learned that it was an option for parents to attend. We supported his decision for us not to not attend the grade 9 orientation. He allowed us to even take his picture, which was never allowed, and wished him a fun-filled day. So far the day was off to a great start. No complaints here until I got a text from my son around 11:30 a.m., which read, "Time is of essence," and he asked if I could make my way down to the school before noon, because of the fact that it would be beneficial to him, being that he would be able to get his timetable and schedule before the first day of school. I arrived at his high school, and just after having entered the main foyer, I saw my son coming out of the auditorium. We greeted each other, and as he continued on with his high school tour, I proceeded to the main office to seek direction in paying his fee.

I was taken to the area where the payments were being accepted; however, upon doing so, I sighted a familiar face that turned out to be a high school friend who is actually a chemistry and special education teacher at my son's new high school. We chatted about old times and then said our goodbyes.

As I walked down the hallway, I felt that all was well. I decided to wait for my son in the main foyer. I sat among a few people, and during the conversations that transpired, we spoke about so many things, but what stood out the most to me is when my new friend asked me if I knew the song "It Is Well." My reply was that it is one of my most favorite gospel songs and that I listen to it every day. She herself could not believe the direction this conversation was going, but again I heard this voice silently whispering, "It is well." Things can happen accidently, but this takes the cake, I remember thinking. From our previous discussion, she knew that I was an educator. She searched her phone diligently, then passed it to me and said that I should read it out loud being that I was a teacher. As I read this story, it became all too familiar to me. I had come across the said story some months ago. The moral of the story was that HE is perfect and is never wrong. But what I did not know about one of my favorite songs is that the composer was a Christian lawyer who went through many atrocities in life, but through them all, he believed and said, "*It is well.*" He experienced so many losses, ranging from losing his only son, to his four daughters, his huge estate, and his law firm, yet in the midst of all his trials, tests, and tribulations, he stated that the Lord taught him to say, "It is well."

This day is one of a few that I will never forget for I met a total stranger that reminded me and taught me such an important lesson to life—that no matter what, IT IS WELL.

Rich Thoughts

How has your latter been greater than the last?

_____

_____

_____

_____

_____

_____

_____

_____

_____

_____

_____

_____

Rich Point for Your Day

Today I will look not to the past but to the future.

Life is RICH when you are able to acknowledge that . . .

Seasons represent growth.

Winter, spring, summer, and fall—these seasons are very symbolic to my life and I am thankful that I was able to see and experience the changes of these seasons.

Although the winter seasons are known for its slippery sidewalks and streets that are often riddled with black ice, snow, and more snow, I don't mind the frigid temperature one bit. While some would beg to differ, this season speaks to the dormant stages in one's life, where things are hibernating and are resting before they become renewed. The spring seasons are known for its downpour of rain showers, worms, flowers, and the blooming of leaves and everything associated with growth and therefore is seen as the refreshed stages of one's life.

The summer seasons become symbolic to restoration with oneself in the sense that the warmth of the sun, good times, and the ability to be free excite and make people happier and on a whole friendlier to those they come into contact with on a daily basis.

And who could forget the fall seasons, which are known for the cool, crisp air; bright, bold, and gorgeous colored leaves; thankful moments; and fall jackets. This season speaks to serious changes where you are stripped of everything. What one must keep in mind is that this is most needed in order to become whole once more.

I have experienced all things characteristic to these seasons and have learned from these transitions tremendously and continue to apply them to my daily life. Although the things that have presented themselves to me at times were difficult to face, each season allowed me to grow and to learn.

Rich Thoughts

What is your favorite season and why?

_____
_____
_____
_____
_____
_____
_____
_____
_____
_____
_____
_____

Rich Point for Your Day

Today I will remember that each season is a necessity for my growth. Therefore, I will embrace and celebrate them all.

Life is RICH when you are able to acknowledge that...

Deceit enslaves while honesty liberates.

Little white lies are just as bad as telling a flat-out lie, so why do we participate in this game of deception?

I choose to withhold the truth from my parents so that they would not have to worry anymore for my health or well-being, for the tests, trials, and tribulations that I have attested to and had endured are no secret. The deceit that I carried within my heart created another kind of pain that caused me to become crippled.

I became enslaved and had continued to be enslaved for close to a year, and each second of the day it bothered me that I had kept this very important secret from my parents. I conjured up different conversations so that I would want to have with them about what I really had been going through. We never had them. I wrote them a letter yet never delivered it, all in the name of protecting my parents from the unknown.

It was close to the one-year mark that the most traumatic event had occurred that I had enough courage to speak to my father. I don't know why it was such a big deal, because the type of relationship I had with my parents was not the kind that kept *things* from each other. It felt as if every thing was falling apart. And when I say everything, I mean my emotional well-being. Learning that I was pregnant, hearing the baby's heartbeat, and then no longer being pregnant were the saddest things to experience. Only the doctors, my husband, my son, and my brother knew at that time; no one else knew. And so because others did not know about this, it made situations that much worse. How do you tell the people that you love and who did not know in the first place that I was pregnant that I lost the baby? That to me made the grieving process difficult to bear. And what made it even worse was that my protectors and best friends—my parents—were not there to comfort me. And because of this absence, I suffered and it tormented me day and night, not being able to speak freely with my loved ones who loved me dearly. Deceit enslaved me when I really yearned for honesty to liberate me. I had many discussions with my husband about *telling* my parents. He offered to be there with me just to show his support, and although I agreed to do so, I did otherwise and silenced my dialogue. It was only after a year and a bit that I mustered up enough courage and told my father during a telephone conversation. Even after I told him, all he did was fuss over my well-being and said that he was sorry and that his baby needed to heal. I could not have agreed with him more. I did need to heal not only physically but emotionally, and the first steps in doing so was when honesty liberated me.

Rich Thoughts

When have you been deceitful? Honest?

_____
_____
_____
_____
_____
_____
_____
_____
_____
_____
_____
_____

Rich Point for Your Day

Today I will be aware that deceit leads to corruption and will strive more towards living a life of honesty.

Life is RICH when you are able to acknowledge that . . .

Soft kisses on the nape of your neck are sweeter than nectar.

To experience the sense of togetherness, affinity, rapport, or attachment between husband and wife is the most blessed and beautiful thing any couple could ever ask for. That *closeness* and the communication piece and all the other important and necessary traits needed to have a loving and lasting relationships, in my eyes, are the main ingredients for a successful friendship and amicable marriage.

It is also a given that for whatever reasons, at times there may be either internal or external factors that may cause turbulence and ultimately contribute to the loss of intimacy in any given relationship. However, I am here to proclaim openly that there will always be some sort of interference. However, please remember that, with anything that may enter into your lives, choose to work it out and be prepared to work hard for the betterment for the both of you. Choose to work on the various parts of your relationship that may need some special attention because, in the end, it is worth it.

Family is everything to me. So when my husband and I encountered a rough patch in our marriage, we reevaluated and reflected not only with ourselves on an individual soul-searching level but also as a couple as to why our level of intimacy was going the direction that it was. And I will be the first to say, it was not always an easy thing to do, but one aspect that contributed to the restoration of our intimacy was reinvesting in ourselves as a couple on all levels and also by doing a thirty-day challenge that involved all the physical, emotional, and spiritual things associated with the art of lovemaking.

I could be mad as hell with my husband for uttering something totally preposterous; not only would his actions irritate me but they would give me great displeasure. But as soon as he stood behind me and would gently spin me around and then softly touch me with his lips, that kiss would just about do it for me because all of those angry thoughts I had and felt toward him would quickly dissipate and would leave such a pleasant taste not only on my lips but on my body as if it were sugar or honey. For there is nothing better than the touch of your husband's lips firmly or softly planted on yours.

It was in and around the time when all the other challenges were being introduced to the world; the most recent being the ALS challenge. However, after watching a talk show and listening to a couple speak about why they decided to participate in the thirty-day sex challenge, the idea became more enticing. The wife spoke about that after she and her husband had children, coupled with their busy schedules, which were important to them, sex no longer became their main priority. They had moved away from being a couple who caressed, kissed, and made love frequently to a couple who at times did not even touch each other sometimes for even eight days. So the wife proposed a thirty-day challenge, which in the beginning was a challenge and really took fourteen days to get into it. What appealed to both my husband and I was that it was not just going to include sex but would bring us back to the basics that we had built our relationship on. Whether it was the holding of hands, the opening of car doors, feeding each other, being considerate of each other's feelings, or having candlelit lovemaking sessions, they all brought us back to that place of intimacy, along with the hard work to make it a habit to live each day as if it were just like the first time we met or like the times when his soft kisses on the nape of my neck become sweeter than nectar.

Rich Thoughts

What part of your body do you love to be kissed the most?

_____

_____

_____

_____

_____

_____

_____

_____

_____

_____

Rich Point for Your Day

Today I will remember how important it is to be kissed and to kiss.

Life is RICH when you are able to acknowledge that . . .

There will always be haters.

Negative thoughts, insecurity, anger, and resentment. I never really understood these sharp pangs of jealousy or passionate dislike people would have for someone or why some people would not want others to succeed. I simply do not understand why people, especially women, for that matter, sometimes find it rather difficult to celebrate other women's success or why they can't be happy for others when they have accomplished and achieved what they have set out to do. I will never fully understand what triggers these feelings of insecurities that other women would display. As a child in elementary school, my mother warned me about having too many female comrades. It did not take me too long to fully comprehend my mother's reasoning behind these words.

There are plenty of *them* that smile in your face and proclaim that they are extremely happy for you, but behind closed doors, their happiness becomes much of a disservice to you. I knew this story oh too well. Whether the so-called friends claimed to be happy for my successes in life, their true feelings became clearer as day. It could be celebrating one of the milestones with my husband and my son, personal growth, spiritual growth, purchasing of a home or a car, or merely my happiness. Truth of this matter is that this behavior could not hide its ugly head from me for too long. For what's in the darkness comes to light. And what hurts the most is that I considered most of these women (that now are a distant memory from my past) as the sisters I never had—the ones whom I confided in and whom I trusted, the ones I thought who were for me and not against me. But you live and you learn to accept the fact that there will always be haters.

I personally believe that this type of behavior or attitude that may develop toward a person or group of people stems from a lack of love from within themselves. They crave to have what you have and crave to be more like you.

Little do they know that what you have required work, hard work. Yes, most things in my life that I had were given to me, but then I also had to work very hard for the things that I have. So when I have fallen victim to this negative emotion, I quickly remember that I don't know what the other person has gone through or what they have experienced to get where they are, because everything that we see is not what it really appears to be. Hence I have made it my duty to celebrate not only my success but other people's successes—genuinely.

I am no longer giving attention to the saying "Your worst enemy can be your best friend, and your friend your worst enemy." I now surround myself around people who are positive, who love to lift others up to higher and unspeakable heights, and more importantly, support other people's dreams and visions. I also surround myself around others who want me to succeed beyond what i may think is my potential, but more importantly, I have come to realize that I no longer want to associate myself with other people's expressions of jealousy because I am not here to be average; I am here to be awesome. So if people don't want to accept that or no longer want to accompany me on my journey, then they should not interrupt those who want to achieve.

Rich Thoughts

What role have you played, the haters or the one being hated on?

_____

_____

_____

_____

_____

_____

_____

_____

_____

_____

_____

_____

_____

Rich Point for Your Day

Today I will remember that the haters have made me famous.

Life is RICH when you are able to acknowledge that . . .

Beauty is in the eye of the beholder.

The Bluffs has always been a special place that I have enjoyed visiting. There is something about nature that allows my mind, body, and spirit to work together that achieves peace.

My father first took my brother and I to the Bluffs when we were young children. He would show us how to select the perfect stone and explain to us the reasons as to why the flat-surfaced ones were the best ones to use. Then he would show us how to position our hands in order to see the result of this stone skipping on the surface of the lake. We would also go for hikes, and when we were tired, we would climb onto one of those huge boulders that sat partially in the lake. Daddy would snap a picture of my brother and I so that my mother would also be able to share the moments that were experienced at the Bluffs. And when we were not resting, if it was a warm day, we would take off our shoes and wade in the water and collect beautiful rocks for our mother, who still has them up until this very day. Those earlier memories with our father at the Bluffs were fun times, especially when he bought us our very own ice cream cones toward the ending of our visit.

Now that I have my own family, the tradition continues to give me great joy and peace when visiting this natural beauty. When my son was younger, he would ride his bike down the bike trails and participate in the same things that I did when I was his age. My husband and I extended those visits to the Bluffs by including barbeques, romantic walks while holding hands, and occasionally ordering food and going to the other side of the Bluffs where the beach was situated. We would sit at a picnic table in the sand as we looked out toward the infinite lake.

Many would say that it is just a huge body of water surrounded by trees and boulders, and it is only for people who engage in either barbequing or who were going for a stroll, and maybe so. But for me, this place will forever be a gem within the city that I can take refuge in and where I can appreciate the gifts from Mother Nature by snapping photographs either of myself or with my family. For we all know, that beauty is in the eye of the beholder.

There was a time when I was unable to visit the Bluffs due to the driving anxieties that I had developed after my motor vehicle accident. I did not want to be in a car, much less travel on the roads, to get to destinations that I had so longed to visit in my mind. However, with time, like everything else, that too became a distant memory and I was able to visit this magnificent place that I missed so much. The first time that I visited the Bluffs was when my husband suggested that we have a mini date. We got a bite to eat and then made our way down to our spot. We talked, we walked, we laughed and held hands, and we spent time together in complete admiration for what surrounded us. It may sound simple to some, but for me that day signified the beauty of being able to lean into the wind and push among the beauty of nature.

Rich Thoughts

What are some of the things that you consider to be beautiful?

_____

_____

_____

_____

_____

_____

_____

_____

_____

_____

_____

_____

_____

Rich Point for Your Day

Today I will search for things that others would deem ugly and find the beauty in them all.

Life is RICH when you are able to acknowledge that . . .

Pillow talks are most needed.

As I get older, I have come to realize that exhaustion comes with the territory of living in a society that constantly rushes at whatever that needs to be done.

We rush to eat breakfast, rush to get to work, and rush to get settled in at our job. Then we rush to *find* the time to eat, rush to get back to work, then rush some more to get home and have things prepared on time to eat dinner as a family, and then rush yet some more to also spend some *quality time* with them. If we are not careful of constantly rushing to do these things, this can and will definitely lead to a burnout. I know this, because I speak from firsthand experience.

Human relaxation is the key to optimal health, for if we do not take the time to do so, the results of such neglect will not be beneficial to you or to your loved ones. Sometimes I would be so tired, unable to fall asleep. Most of the time I was not to blame for the inability to fall asleep and stay asleep. The melodic snores of my husband were the number one culprit for keeping me awake; the constant elbowing and pinching of this man in order to try to get him to sleep on his side kept me wide awake and rather busy. If I was not busy doing that, then I was awakened to the constant turning and rolling over of my husband. At times it is as if I was watching a synchronized swimming event with the amount of twists and turns he did in a small given amount of time. At some point in time, my body would decide to surrender to the most needed sleep, and my pillow that cushioned my head and other parts of my body allowed me, even for a few hours, to appreciate uninterrupted sleep. As the night turned into weeks, then into months and then sadly into years, the inability to sleep lead to more pressing issues, particularly that of worry. Things had changed drastically from the time of my motor vehicle accident. Posttraumatic stress, anxiety, and depression kicked in—not by choice. However, not being able to identify these illnesses made it that much harder. However, once I was able to medically identify the reasons for my inability to sleep. I was able to pinpoint the underlying causes, work through them, and then move forward. Once I was able to do the things that I once loved, relax, and regain the pieces of my life that had been lost. My pillow began to befriend me again, and I realized how these pillow talks were missed.

Rich Thoughts

When are the times that you have spoken to your pillow the most?

_____

_____

_____

_____

_____

_____

_____

_____

_____

_____

_____

_____

_____

Rich Point for Your Day

Today I will not ignore the times when my pillow needs to speak to me.

Life is RICH when you are able to acknowledge that . . .

Smiles are contagious.

About 99 percent of the time a complete stranger will return the smile that I have given them. Whether they return it out of obligation or under the mere assumption that I may be flirting with them, they do end up returning the smile. Personally, I just think that that the real reason as to why the smiles are returned is because I personally believe that they are simply contagious and usually spread like wildfire to others.

Yes, occasionally I will get the odd crusty individual who chooses to continue frowning as opposed to reciprocating the smile, but I continue doing what I love to do smile.

Sometimes a smile is all a person really needs to see or receive in order to break the shackles and chains of despair that they may be facing in their lives. I know that when someone smiles at me, it automatically triggers an amused facial expression despite the way I may be feeling on that given day. Or when I see someone smiling as opposed to not, I choose to imitate what I've already saw. If you practice doing it on a daily basis, it becomes force of habit and second nature to you. There was a point in time that my life had gently wiped those smiles away and completely replaced them with a frown. The pressures of life had gotten to me, more ways than one, and as each day progressed, it became difficult to partake in something that I loved until I became more cognizant of the woman who seemed to always have a smile planted on her face.

I observed her intently to see if she would slip up when having to deal with an irate customer. But she never did; she continued to wear her smile proudly to the point that I decided to ask her the next time I saw her if she had always displayed such a pleasant manner. She replied yes, and so because of her, I too decided that I would never let anything get me down to the point where it would negotiate my right to be happy or smile. So because of her contagious smile, I too smile 'cause I have every right too.

Rich Thoughts

What makes you smile?

_____

_____

_____

_____

_____

_____

_____

_____

_____

_____

_____

_____

_____

Rich Point for Your Day

Today I will remember that smiles are contagious, and therefore I will smile more today.

Life is RICH when you are able to acknowledge that . . .

Respect is like an umbrella.

An umbrella has many purposes. Not only does this device consist of a circular canopy of cloth that has a folding metal frame, the umbrella is supported by a central rod and can also be used as some form of protection against either the rain or the sun. All in all it remains to be an important protective force.

Respect is also quite symbolic to the functioning of the umbrella with the respects of them both being a protecting force. What I mean here is that, if you do not have respect, everything that defines you may begin to disintegrate.

Creating a relationship with yourself and having one with others are very important to plant, nurture, and grow. For when one respects themselves, they work hard to continue loving themselves, take pride in themselves, and view the world differently and hence protect themselves in doing so. Having respect for others also intends for you to work hard by continuing to love them the best way you know, which in turn allows one the ability to listen and learn while working on being mindful of not only your words, actions, and thoughts but theirs too.

For when these things are not fulfilled or followed, there will be absolute chaos. End of story.

However, many beg to differ and believe that it is their right to get everything they want.

Not quite sure how I came up with the analogy of the umbrella and comparing it to the concept of respect, but I did and I have been using it in my classroom every academic school year ever since I became an educator. It worked well. Because the students could visualize the umbrella, it made it that easier to address issues of respect and have them abide by these rules. It became part of the classroom and part of their lives for it taught them that, in order to gain that they must earn. It also taught them to take responsibility for their actions for they could be held accountable for these actions if need be. These life lessons taught them that respect encompasses everything they say and do.

Rich Thoughts

Why is respect such an important ingredient to add to one's life?

_____
_____
_____
_____
_____
_____
_____
_____
_____
_____
_____
_____
_____

Rich Point for Your Day
Today I will be respectful of others, my property, and myself.

Life is RICH when you are able to acknowledge that . . .

Attitude determines altitude.

My attitude has not always been up to par, for at times, it was less than joyous, and instead of me reaping the benefits to the things that I had set out to accomplish, my visions remained where I had first left them, at the very beginning stages. And I only had myself to blame.

The saying "Your attitude determines your altitude" is a phrase that I try to live by. And although I have great intentions, at times I have fallen short of these *simple yet complex* instructions. When you think of these few words, they make all the sense in the world, and if you are able to live by them, well, they make even better sense to learn how to apply them to your daily life.

Although easier said than done, I found that each day the habit to have my attitude coincide with my altitude equipped me with the tools I needed to aim higher and accomplish what I initially intended to do. We even extended this invite to our son and reminded him daily that, if his thinking or feeling about someone or something was low, that is exactly how high he would go as far as the things he set out to do. However, if his attitude was high, he would soar higher than any eagle and possibly surpass his expectations of either tackling or completing a task.

I am still a work in progress and continue to be for the rest of my life, because I am a human being and will make mistakes. However, being able to admit this and continuing to strive for the best will allow me to conquer anything with confidence and positivity.

Rich Thoughts

When has your attitude been less than joyous?

_____

_____

_____

_____

_____

_____

_____

_____

_____

_____

_____

_____

Rich Point for Your Day

Today my attitude will be so high that not even the eagles soaring in the sky can reach me.

Life is RICH when you are able to acknowledge that . . .

You deserve a top of a morning.

Have a top of a morning, my father told me. When I heard those words uttered from his mouth, I quickly ran for my pen and paper and asked him to repeat that phrase one more time so that I may jot it down and add to the many phrases that I have grown to love and use on a daily basis.

I liked the way that those words sounded and therefore decided that it would be nice to also share a similar message to all my friends and family members that morning.

My father always spoke with such wisdom and always allowed you to think about your thinking. So I too decided to take those words and run with them. For when you really think about a person being on top, it really does mean that they are at the highest level they could possibly be placed.

How fitting my father's words had become, because it seemed as if life had been dishing out many hard balls as of late and, to say the least, things had gotten a bit overwhelming. Our home had been sold, my family and I seemed we were living here and living there yet still breathing in the midst of our chaos, and in doing so, it began to take its toll on everyone, and all I ever wanted was just an ounce of normalcy in my life. So hearing my father say these words, little did he know, or maybe he did, they were quite appropriate and much needed to be heard right there and then. My father always had a way with words and always spoke logic and truth. I love my conversations with him and learned from each and every one more than he will ever know. He's an awesome man, father, friend, and teacher and I am so grateful that I was so blessed to have him in my life.

From that day forward, either I have told others that they deserve a top of a morning or I have taken my father's advice for myself, because I have learned that at the end of the day life is too short and we deserve to be the best and only the best in everything that we do. I worked hard to get where I am today. I worked extremely hard to overcome the atrocities associated with that wretched car accident and everything associated with it, so yes, I do deserve to have a top of a morning, afternoon, and evening—as you all do too!

Rich Thoughts

How do you make your mornings most worthwhile?

_____

_____

_____

_____

_____

_____

_____

_____

_____

_____

_____

_____

Rich Point for Your Day

Today I will have a top of the morning and will let nothing hinder me from doing so.

Life is RICH when you are able to acknowledge that . . .

We don't have to do everything.

Because I was always able to juggle and maintain the role of wearing the hat of an emotional specialist so well, I was always expected to do so. Hence I was always being placed on that pedestal because, no matter what, anything and everything that was ever passed my way was done close to perfection.

I gave everything, my all, and never settled for second best. Hence the reasoning behind being given the *she can do it* because I always did. It was only after having a conversation with my sister-in-law about how, as women, we tend to wear so many hats and fulfill these roles quite close to perfection. The expectation and notion that more is better becomes attached to women. We have always been capable to *just do it* so naturally that the self-fulfilling prophecy became our truth and belief that *we* have to do everything! She told me that we don't have to do everything, and if there are dishes in the sink or the laundry is not completed or if dinner is not eaten at a certain time, then that's okay! What she was professing sounded a bit right, but it had been ingrained in my mind, especially seeing not only my grandmothers do this but my mother do this, and since children learn what they see, I ended up doing it too!

But as time went on, I did cave in—well, just a little—and lived by the words of my sister-in-law and did what *I* could do. The guilt of not having it done on time no longer bothered me as it did before because I know and my family knew that I was not a lazy person. My husband and my son did, however, start to participate in *helping* out in and around out home, which made things a lot better for me and literally lightened up my once-heavy load. For they too realized the importance of being able to live a life that was conducive to change and welcomed and appreciated the fact that having a balance is more than necessary, but more importantly, they also realized that I don't have to do everything.

Whoever came up with the idea that the men are supposed to be the economic providers while the women be the emotional specialists who have to not only attend to the needs of the family, her husband, and children but to do all the "inside" things, better known as the chores, in and around the house is absurd. I believe that both men and women should willingly be able to wear both hats of the economic provider and also the emotional specialist simultaneously. That is how they were worn when I was growing up. My father combed and styled my hair, took care of us, cooked and cleaned, and also worked a nine-to-five job, and my mother did the same. And so naturally, when I had my own family, the helping-each-other syndrome continued. However, at some point in time, the shared roles came to a halt and seemed as if I were the only emotional specialist for myself, husband, and son.

No one seemed to know where anything was anymore, for it seemed that they conveniently had amnesia as to where everything was located. It seemed to me that I was doing more than what I initially bargained for.

Within the past few months, this topic of discussion had also been a household special feature which all pointed to the same findings, me doing most of the cooking and cleaning and taking care of my family's needs and wants. I thought that being off from work would allow me the rest, which everyone was saying that I was in so much need of. However, it just seemed as if those words were just a figment of my imagination.

Rich Thoughts

Name something that you do not enjoy doing.

_____

_____

_____

_____

_____

_____

_____

_____

_____

_____

_____

Rich Point for Your Day

Today I will remind myself throughout the day that I DO NOT have to finish everything.

Life is RICH when you are able to acknowledge that . . .

You rock and you are beautiful.

"Go on with your bad self!" I told myself as I put on my other black, white, and red stilettos. Not only am I intelligent, ambitious, and a creative woman, I am not too hard on the eyes, or so I have been told. So when others tend to want to classify my opinions about how I feel about carrying myself or see me as being too conceited or into myself, this only confirms that, with each passing day, I am becoming more of a rocker and hence more beautiful.

When I speak of being classified as a rocker, I am not speaking of any association with the actual heavy metal person or headbanger who listens to various music artists or plays this particular genre of music. I speak of being that person who has chosen to stand firm in anything that comes their way and therefore as a result, these women become much firmer and more solid and share similar characteristics as a rock. In doing so, this is not necessarily a very easy thing to do, but gathering strength during those particular trying times and then being able to see the beauty in them make you a die-hard rocker.

I can't speak for anyone else. However, all I have ever known was to be a beautiful rocker. Therefore, it was only second nature to act, speak, and think as one. A friend had said one day that no one would ever have known the things that I have endured just by *looking at me*. When I asked her what she meant, she found great difficulty explaining herself in regards to her statement but later replied by saying that the difference between myself and the other people whom she knew that had trials and tribulations and have experienced so much tests in their lives was that my mountains, so to speak, all happened within such a short period of time. She continued to say that she could not fathom how my soul managed to still be very much alive after having gone through so many right after the other.

My response to my friend was that I give thanks to the Almighty Father for seeing me through those rough patches in my life and am most humbled to know that he was so gracious to me to lean on him when I no longer felt strong. I continuously give thanks to HIM for allowing me to fall but also give thanks to HIM for guiding me through my journey. This, I explained to my friend, refined me into that *beautiful rocker* because of HIM, and his hands always outstretched toward me. I always seemed to get right back up again and stand on that rock of courage and determination.

So don't you ever think it can't be done, and don't you ever think that you are not beautiful, for just as a diamond goes through a process where it must withstand a lot of heat and pressure, you do too! Conditions need to be perfect to make the adequate carbon bonds into a diamond, just as your situations will make you stronger.

Rich Thoughts

How do you rock?

_____

_____

_____

_____

_____

_____

_____

_____

_____

_____

_____

_____

_____

Rich Point for Your Day

Today I will continue to Rock on with my bad ass self!

Life is RICH when you are able to acknowledge that . . .

Life should give off fragrance.

I have a few selected perfumes that I have been adding to my personal collection throughout the years, and I must say that I have grown to absolutely love them all.

Their smells are rather delightful and also very pleasing to the senses. Who doesn't like to get all dolled up, have their makeup looking like you've stepped out of the page of a *Vogue* magazine, and effortlessly smell seductively sexy.

Misting a hint of my favorite perfume behind the earlobes, along the nape of my neck, and on my wrists is so very tasteful to me. However, if you overdo the misting of these scents, like anything in your life, it becomes overbearing and at times can be stifling.

Life is very much like the misting of your favorite perfume. When you do things, say things, and think of things to better your life, the rewards can bring only in positivity and ultimately bring forth good to your life.

It was approximately a year after we had sold our property. Our intention was to move into a particular area; however, things did not pan out the way we had intended it to be. We lived among family members and occasionally in hotels for almost a year. During those times, many things became hectic and the things that used to give off a sweet fragrance no longer did. However, in the midst of our relocation, we humbled ourselves, continued to give thanks in everything that we did, and prayed for the best despite the fact that it would appear to the naked eye as if all odds had been stacked against us. Funny enough, last year around this time when we were shopping around for a place to call home, our son expressed the emotional attachment that he had when entering into an area in which we had wanted to reside. We all felt this way. However, as my father would always say, every disappointment is for a reason, and so it was.

It was the month of June when we had contacted a few Realtors. One in particular from the very beginning mirrored the exact words that my father had spoken—what's yours is YOURS—and reassured us not to worry.

Life seemed to be on the up-and-up and smelled quite good. Good in the sense that the sweet-smelling fragrances were once again filling up every area of our lives and there was no longer an offensive odor with the fragrances we chose to wear. I believe that it was attributed to us remaining in a positive frame of mind despite the challenges that we had to face.

We continued on with our day believing that all would be well and everything would be restored, although at times this was a very difficult thing to practice. We practiced and practiced not giving up because practices makes purpose, and our purpose was to accept the various kinds of fragrances that had been misted on us, even when we did not want to accept it. But we did, and now we are living at that exact location that we had viewed prior to the shifts in our lives. We live in a home that was intended for us. All the overbearing and stifling scents were worth testing, for if it were not for them, how would we have ever known how beautiful the fragrance of life could be?

Rich Thoughts

Name a perfume that best suits the fragrance of your life.

Rich Point for Your Day

Today I will allow my fragrance of life to fill any room with a sweet smell.

Life is RICH when you are able to acknowledge that . . .

Contentment makes us RICH.

Funny enough, if you were to ask me a question about what makes me happy or content when I was a teenager, I think making loads of money and having an endless amount of it would be my ideal answer where being content is concerned.

However, having had the opportunity to make loads of money and in that process being able to *grow wiser* have allowed me to reevaluate the importance of what really makes me content. Needless to say, I have changed my answer in my adult years, and I would have to say that my current thought to that question is that I am most content with the not-so-grandiose things of life.

For I have found a deeper appreciation for this state of happiness or satisfaction that is present in my life. I now know that I want to continue living this way because there are so many benefits in doing so.

However, there was a time when this state of happiness or satisfaction that I speak so highly of became void from my life despite the fact that I had been surrounded by love and kindness.

The things that gave me pleasure, whether it be from a materialistic or personal point of view, no longer served their purpose. Hanging with my friends, traveling, going for secret rendezvous with my husband, going shopping, driving long distances, and even attending family functions became a chore that I had to muster up an enormous amount of energy that conjured up moments of unnecessary anxiety. I'd rather be alone, and when I was not alone, I pretended to be happy when the truth is that I was not.

Something had taken over, and the new me said good-bye to the old me. However, during this transformation, my priorities changed back to the basics. It switched from wanting to make money and receive a huge paycheck and balancing out my family life to wanting everything encompassed around being happy with my family.

I redefined my understanding of what it means to be rich in my quiet moments. I no longer equated richness with the acquisition of wealth, the fancy cars, the haute couture clothing, or weekend getaways in a posh resort. For I discovered the real meaning of what it means to be rich—it means to be whole and therefore giving precedence to being balanced in body, mind, and spirit. Being rich means to be satisfied to be thankful for what you have and being content watching the sunrise or the sunset or watching the moon and the stars above. And in that redefinition, I too redefined who I was. I was no longer that busy person easily distracted. I now became and realized that I am like the sand in the sea—immeasurably rich.

Rich Thoughts

What makes you RICH?

_____

_____

_____

_____

_____

_____

_____

_____

_____

_____

_____

_____

Rich Point for Your Day

Today I will focus on continuing to be mindful of what I sow.

CPSIA information can be obtained at www.ICGtesting.com
Printed in the USA
LVOW08s2355270415

436304LV00001B/9/P